Conversations with
SAMUEL WILSON, JR.

Conversations with
SAMUEL WILSON, JR.

Dean of Architectural Preservation in New Orleans

Edited by
Abbye A. Gorin

Forewords by
Ronald C. Filson
& Ann Masson

A Louisiana Landmarks Society Book

PELICAN PUBLISHING COMPANY
GRETNA 2012

Published by arrangement with the Louisiana Landmarks Society by
Pelican Publishing Company, Inc., 2012

First printing, 1991
Second printing, 1991
First Pelican edition, 2011

*The word "Pelican" and the depiction of a pelican
are trademarks of Pelican Publishing Company, Inc.,
and are registered in the U.S. Patent and Trademark Office.*

Library of Congress Catalog Card Number 91-065072
ISBN 9781589809864

Front-cover photograph by Abbye A. Gorin

Printed in the United States of America
Published by Pelican Publishing Company, Inc.
1000 Burmaster Street, Gretna, Louisiana 70053

To our ability to assess the past and present so that we can anticipate the future.

Contents

LIST OF ILLUSTRATIONS

x

Fig. 3. Delord-Sarpy House, 1955.

Anyone desiring
to study America's historic buildings
can find an immense quantity of books on the
subject, but this literature includes very
little material on the history of the people
who have saved these buildings
for posterity.

— Charles B. Hosmer, Jr.

Fig. 4. Madame John's Legacy, 1930.

FOREWORD

This volume, the second by Ms. Gorin regarding the life and works of Samuel Wilson, Jr., offers new and insightful information to the reader interested in topics related to Historic Preservation, the Architecture of New Orleans, Architectural Education in the twentieth century, and the professional life of a fascinating architect.

Ms. Gorin's earlier work, "Samuel Wilson, Jr.: A Contribution to the Preservation of Architecture in New Orleans and the Gulf South," a dissertation on the work of Wilson completed in 1989 at Virginia Polytechnic Institute and State University, explored a wide range of projects and the research undertaken by Wilson during his career. This volume offers a much more intimate glimpse of what was involved in carrying out all that research and executing all of those projects so carefully delineated.

As is usual, this makes for probably a much more fascinating and readable book.

In conducting her research for her dissertation and this volume, the author has been able to conduct numerous interviews with the subject, Sam Wilson, and with many involved with his work during his career. As a result, she has been able to expose many of the intricate and complex workings of the architectural profession and the hundreds of tasks, steps, phases, and complications involved in any architectural project, especially those which necessitate historical research and adaptation for their execution.

Abbye Gorin's first association with Sam Wilson dates to 1961 when she took his Louisiana Architecture course. Sam Wilson has had a long and extremely successful teaching career at Tulane University (thirty-eight years beginning in 1946) where he influenced three generations of would-be architects, preservationists, historians, and dutiful citizens interested in their city. Ms. Gorin's research laid the ground work for a tremendously well received nomination for the honorary degree that was conferred upon Sam Wilson in 1990.

The importance of this work is not to be underestimated both in terms of its documentation of Sam Wilson's career, or perhaps more importantly, its ability to put the efforts and the work of one man along (with his associates and professional colleagues) into a larger cultural and professional context at work throughout the twentieth century. Sam Wilson's career spans a most significant period of architectural thought from the 1930s until today, and as a result of Ms. Gorin's work, we understand much better the forces at work and the possible interpretations and reactions to them made by architects over the last fifty years.

Any single research effort and publication is but one tile in the mosaic of culture and thought. This is an important piece of the fabric and a work that will help us know and appreciate the achievements of a significant figure of the twentieth century and better understand our culture and its efforts to express itself physically.

Ronald C. Filson
Dean, School of Architecture
Tulane University

Foreword

Conversations with Sam Wilson were always a pleasure. With his courtly manner, dry wit, and encyclopedic knowledge, he shared his love of architecture with anyone wise enough to listen. Generations of students attended his acclaimed Louisiana architecture classes, which were filled to overflowing for decades. Many had never studied the built environment, but each left the classroom with a newfound appreciation of the extraordinary collection of historic buildings that is New Orleans. Sam's love of the city manifested beyond the classroom—in restorations and writings, in research and advocacy, and in private and professional life. This small volume encapsulates his thoughts on many aspects of his career and the buildings and lives he touched.

Sam's scholarship began as a student at what is now Tulane University's School of Architecture, from which he graduated in 1931 when the country was in the depth of the Great Depression. During his freshman year, his interest in historic buildings was sparked by a project to complete measured drawings of three French Quarter doorways. He went on to make sketches and watercolors of important structures, a complement to his study of architectural theory and history with Nathaniel Cortlandt Curtis (1881-1953), Tulane's first full-time architectural educator. Jobs for newly minted architects were scarce, but Wilson found employment with Curtis and Moise Goldstein (1882-1972), one of the city's premier architects.

In 1933, as part of the Works Progress Administration initiative to end the economic crisis, the Historic American Buildings Survey was created. A joint project of the National Park Service, the American Institute of Architects, and the Library of Congress, the program engaged architects throughout the country to make measured drawings of historic buildings. HABS, as it is still known, brought Wilson into the office of architect and project district officer Richard Koch (1889-1971), with whom he formed a partnership in 1955. Koch and Wilson Architects remains one of the region's most respected specialists in historic architecture.

While researching, measuring, and examining the finest buildings of Louisiana's past, Wilson developed an abiding enthusiasm for the forms and history of these treasures, many of which are now gone or irreparably altered. He traveled the state with Richard Koch, whose evocative photographs are perhaps the finest images of early Louisiana buildings captured at the moment just before they were overtaken by change. Thus Wilson's knowledge was based on an intimate relationship with the buildings themselves, an experience only rarely possible today. He coupled this insight with an archivist's love of historical research. He read old newspapers at the Howard Library near Lee Circle, discovered the treasure trove of drawings in the Notarial Archives, and began exhaustive research in old records, often taking notes on small rectangles of white paper. Combined with his architectural ability, these experiences were the basis of Wilson's later work in restoration, design, and writing.

Remaining in Koch's office, Wilson gradually assumed more responsibility for a new project—the reshaping of City Park, for which the firm designed bridges and other structures. In 1938, he received an AIA travel scholarship that enabled him to venture abroad for the first time. A visit to the French Colonial archives, then housed in Paris, brought an astounding discovery. There among the thousands of documents were original drawings sent from Louisiana by eighteenth-century French military engineers— depictions of buildings that had long ago disappeared in fires and hurricanes and demolitions. An important find was that the Ursuline Convent, the only remaining French Colonial building in New Orleans, was not the one completed in 1734, as had always been assumed, but another built in 1750 to replace the earlier, crumbling building. His European trip, colorfully recounted in this volume, inspired the young architect to begin a serious study of the architecture of Colonial Louisiana. Wilson wrote on many other aspects of Louisiana's history, and he skillfully edited two journals by nineteenth-century architects—Benjamin Latrobe and T. K. Wharton. The list at the end of this volume guides the reader to his published works, an impressive body of scholarship that remains the bedrock for today's studies.

This is only one aspect of a legendary career that spanned six decades. As a restoration architect, he worked on many notable buildings, including the Cabildo, Hermann-Grima House, Gallier House, Ursuline Convent, San Francisco Plantation, and Shadows-on-the-Teche, to name only a few. He lectured widely, hosted a television show about local architecture, served on innumerable boards and committees, and consistently advocated for the preservation of historic Louisiana. In 1949, he helped found the Louisiana Landmarks Society, still housed in the building he worked to save—the Pitot House—and served as president for six years. The lists of architectural works, civic involvement, and honors bestowed by grateful organizations comprise another useful section of this volume.

When the "Dean of Historic Preservation" in New Orleans died in his Garden District home, he was involved in fighting the 1993 demolition of a landmark of the modern era, the Rivergate (1969), which stood at the foot of Canal Street where Harrah's Casino is today. Some were surprised by the eighty-two-year-old's enthusiasm for such a recent structure, but Wilson was not limited in his approach to preservation. Part of his training had been in modern design, and he appreciated good buildings from any era. While he could be exacting in a restoration, he was not always a purist. He knew that not every building could be saved. He understood how to be sensitive in adapting buildings to new purposes, and he was interested in preserving the character of old neighborhoods years before it became fashionable.

The beauty of *Conversations with Samuel Wilson, Jr.* is that its candid tone reveals his opinions about historic preservation, along with unique insights into issues and projects. One conversation recounts how the granite piers of the old St. Louis Hotel came to be preserved on the Chartres Street side of the Royal Orleans

Hotel. Another discusses the demolition and rebuilding of the Spanish Colonial Orue-Pontalba House. The conversations touch on the history of local preservation efforts, document details of important projects, and present a preservation point of view that remains relevant. Concerning the current topic of infill in older neighborhoods, Wilson states with characteristic directness, "New architecture in old areas, I don't think it should be anything exotic, ought to be simple and direct, good proportions, good design."

The book was first published in 1991, when one could just call Mr. Wilson and ask his opinion about a building or a bit of research or a preservation issue. He was always generous with his time and patient in his responses. His curiosity about architecture never waned, although it was nearly impossible to find something he had not already seen. With kindness, he mentored a generation of preservationists who are still carrying on the work of saving buildings and preserving neighborhoods. Reading *Conversations with Samuel Wilson, Jr.* is like having him in the room offering history, philosophy, and wit in his humble and gracious way.

Ann M. Masson

Fig. 5. Perspective view of Latrobe's U.S. Custom House, 1954.

ACKNOWLEDGMENTS

One of Mr. Wilson's outstanding characteristics is his willingness to share his research. It is in the Wilson spirit of sharing that I proposed *Conversations* to the Samuel Wilson, Jr. Publications Fund of the Louisiana Landmarks Society. My gratitude to the Board for their commitment to publish this manuscript.

To Friends of the Cabildo Oral History Program for permission to publish portions of Dorothy G. Schlesinger's excellent conversations she had with Mr. Wilson.

To the bookmaking crew, Dr. S. Steven Gorin, my husband, for his computer technical assistance in the four programs that were used in the writing and production of this book and for his help in computer typesetting the text; Franklin Adams for his cover design and art direction; Rhoda Seligmann for her portrait of Mr. Wilson; Helen Malin for copy editing; Dr. Wilbur E.

Meneray for serving as critic and for his help in computer typesetting the text. To John Geiser III and Elizabeth Wolf for proofreading.

To William R. Cullison III, curator of the Southeastern Architectural Archive, Linda Poe and Helen Burkes, library assistants in Special Collections — all at the Tulane University Library — for their help in the detail work of research. And to Eric Palladini, Jr., graduate assistant in Special Collections at Tulane, for his help in generating this computerized, camera-ready manuscript.

To Ronald C. Filson, Dean of the School of Architecture, Tulane for his support of *Conversations* when it was only an idea and his contribution of the Foreword.

And to Mr. Wilson, a special thanks for the many conversations that it has taken to sort out his career thus far.

Fig. 6. Dufilho House, 1930.

INTRODUCTION

The official founding date of Louisiana Landmarks Society, 1950, marks the institutionalization of historic preservation in New Orleans. The founding president was Samuel Wilson, Jr. This event, actually an outgrowth of Wilson's first class in Louisiana Architecture (1946), signified his clear leadership of the New Orleans family of preservationists — a position he held for the next twenty years. Wilson's influence has been felt locally and regionally, especially in the area of Natchez, Mississippi. He is also part of the larger national circle of architects, academics, and administrators who coalesced scattered pockets of preservation activity in America into a national movement.

Although Wilson perceives himself simply as an architect, he has conducted his career in three realms simultaneously — practicing architect, scholar, and civic leader. If one laid out

Wilson's career in a linear manner, it would appear that he was always the right man in the right place, at the right time, with the right set of skills. He was perhaps lucky, but more probably, it was his position in the sequence of an architectural and social phenomenon that presented the opportunities for him to develop his talents.

Wilson entered Tulane University in 1927. The classical tradition — derived from the French Ecole des Beaux-Arts, the root of American architectural teaching philosophy — was near the end of its life cycle and a new cycle was in bloom, modernism. Wilson was trained in this overlapping period of change, and as a result, he worked in both schools of thought, the old and the new. The old French Quarter of New Orleans, also called the Vieux Carré, was his laboratory where he began to build his vocabulary of eighteenth and nineteenth century Creole forms and to develop an appreciation for old buildings, the people who created them, and the use of these old structures. At the same time, he also admired the work of the modernists.

About 1929 a renaissance began to save the old French Quarter. Three architects who were instrumental in the creation of this interest were Nathaniel Cortlandt Curtis, Moise H. Goldstein, and Richard Koch. They were the trio of architectural minds who taught, inspired, and employed Wilson. The Koch and Wilson relationship, which began as prodigy to mentor, developed into a collaborative team. In large measure it was the work of Richard Koch and Samuel Wilson, Jr. Architects that made New Orleans a respectable center of historic preservation in the United States.

By an examination of the coming together of the old and the new in Wilson's career, one can define the very meaning of the modern preservation movement. It is where a new use is found for an old building; new technology and new materials are used to repair an old building; new designs are created out of old parts; old designs are reconstructed with new materials, and old forms are perpetuated in modern buildings.

The old and the new came together in Wilson's life during the Great Depression (1931) when he participated in the Historic American Buildings Survey (HABS) — the beginning of a collection of a new body of knowledge — a national inventory of historic American buildings in graphic and textual form. Wilson not only perfected his art of measuring and drawing buildings, but he developed research and writing skills to unravel and tell the story of an old structure's life. The HABS experience coupled with his 1938 European travels was the foundation on which he developed his interest in architectural history and historic preservation, both young fields in the 1930s.

The intent of *Conversations* is to allow the dean of architectural preservation in New Orleans to explain in his own words the social milieu out of which he came, some of his philosophies and principles of historic preservation, research methods, and orgins of his designs. The conversations plus the Catalog — Historic Architectural Projects, Literary Works, Honors And Awards — demonstrate the breadth of the historic side of Wilson's practice which includes new designs with an historic memory.

Conversations offers the reader an experience of a simulated personal contact with this quiet and unassuming architect. In an effort to preserve Mr. Wilson's down-home personality through his speech, *Conversations* has been edited only for clarity. Notes, inserts, and examples of Mr. Wilson's documentary architectural art have been added to enrich these vignettes. For reading ease all historic buildings are printed in bold type. Included in the Bibliography are Suggested References to guide the reader to some New Orleans resources as well as general information concerning the modern preservation movement. This work is derived from the author's dissertation "Samuel Wilson, Jr.: A Contribution to the Preservation of Architecture in New Orleans and the Gulf South."

Conversations is about a native son who has made a substantial contribution to saving our architectural heritage for posterity. This book is, in reality, a chapter in the history of American architecture.

Part One

MEET MR. WILSON

Fig. 7. Rhoda Seligmann, drawing, Samuel Wilson, Jr., 1985.

MEET MR. WILSON

I never knew where the Vieux Carré was until I was practically out of high school. We didn't call it the Vieux Carré, we called it the French Quarter. I'd never even been near the place. My mother was always interested in the opera. When the Opera House burned, she was all in a tizzy. My father said, "The whole place ought to burn down. It would be the best thing that could happen for the city."

— Samuel Wilson, Jr.[1]

Biographical Facts

Schlesinger:[2] The Friends of the Cabildo Oral History Program is an on-going project which compiles cultural history by means of interviews recorded on audio tapes. We would like to hear recollections of your way of life, significant people in your life, interesting occurances. Let's begin with some biographical information. Please tell us when you were born and give some family background.

Wilson: I was born in New Orleans August 6, 1911. My father's family had been in New Orleans since 1824. My great grandfather, who was Samuel Wilson, was a native of Ireland. He was born in 1799. He was only twenty-five when he came to New Orleans. I don't know if he had been here before, but when I edited Benjamin H. B. Latrobe's New Orleans Impressions, his journals (Wilson 1951), among the passengers on the ship with Latrobe coming to New Orleans in 1819 was Samuel Wilson.[3] If it was my great grandfather or not, I've always been curious.

My great grandfather was in the wholesale meat business, and he had a place in the French Market.[4] It was advertised on the cover of some of the city directories in the 1840s and 1850s.

My father was born here also. He went to the University of the South at Sewanee, Tennessee and Tulane. He graduated in law at Tulane. Unfortunately, he only practiced for a short time. Things would have been much better if he had remained with the law instead of in business.

My mother was born in St. Paul, Minnesota. When they were first married, they lived in Chicago where my brother was born. Then they came back here and built a house at 7730 Burthe Street. The house is still there. We lived there until about 1925, when I was in high school.

I went to school at what was then McDonogh 23 on the corner of Carrollton Avenue and Maple Street, which was a Greek Revival building by the architect Henry Howard.[5] It had been the old **Carrollton Courthouse.**[6] I had very good teachers. I skipped two half grades, and when I was twelve years old, I went to Warren Easton High School which was the only public boys' high school in the city. It was quite some distance away. I'd usually take the streetcar. The St. Charles-Tulane belt car ran all the way around in those days. I used to take books along to read.

I never seemed to study much. I don't think it was required. One of the earliest things that affected me was joining the Boy Scouts. My father was always interested in politics, although he never really participated. He used to take me out to political meetings. I remember hearing Huey Long's harangue.[7] In those days we didn't have radio or TV reports on election returns, so we'd walk over to the corner store. I remember going over to a store on Carrollton and Poplar, which is now Willow Street. They would post the returns on the glass on the front window of the store. It was the mayor's race between Martin Behrman, the old line politician, and Andrew J. McShane, the reform candidate.[8] We went to hear the election returns and ran into Mr. Charles Macmurdo, an old friend of my father's, and who happened to be a Scout Master of Troop 46 at the St. Charles Avenue Presbyterian Church.

My mother, brother, sisters, and I were Catholics. We went to Mater Delorosa Church on Carrollton Avenue. Mr. Macmurdo gave me such a sales talk that I went over and joined his scout troop. I think I was thirteen. I enjoyed it very much. I became an Assistant Scout Master, because nobody else would do it, then Scout Master because nobody else would. About 1933 a Sea Scout unit started. I think a lot of boys who were in the program with me or under me, many of them I am still very friendly with, knew me as a Sea Scout leader rather than an architect. I took a bunch of my Sea Scouts to a Scout Jamboree in Washington in 1937. Some of us went on to Williamsburg at that time. I took another bunch up to the New York World's Fair in '39.

Schlesinger: Did you always envision going into architecture?

Wilson: Yes. I don't know how I knew what an architect was but when I was a kid, I used to like to build model cities and model houses. We had a set of books, the *Book of Knowledge,* that had patterns for making a model of Ann Hathaway's cottage at Stratford. I'd put these little things together and made villages. I think my mother said, "Maybe you ought to be an architect."

I had a friend, Pete Livaudais, who lived around the corner, whose father was an architect, Mr. L. A. Livaudais of the firm Favrot and Livaudais. My father and I went over and had a chat with him one day to see what would be the best approach to this thing. I was then in high school. Where would be the best place to go to college? Mr. Livaudais said, "I never went to college." He had just grown up in the profession and he said, "Tulane is probably as good a one as any place else."[9] When I finished high school, I went to Tulane. I finished in architecture there in 1931.

Tulane University

Schlesinger: When did you get interested in the Vieux Carré?

Wilson: It was when I got into Tulane that I began to be interested in the Quarter. One of my freshman projects was to make a measured drawing of three doorways. I measured a doorway like the one on Matilda Stream's house but at the next corner, an apartment house now.[10] I drew another doorway on Rampart and St. Peter Streets which is gone. The doorway was ripped out and thrown away. From my drawing I based the doorway I put on Fritz Ingram's house.[11]

In my second year we had to make a study on Louisiana

Fig. 8. Three Doorways from the French Quarter, circa 1928.

architecture for which there was a prize, the Labouisse Prize, that had been established in memory of Mr. S. S. Labouisse of the firm De Buys, Churchill, and Labouisse, who did Holy Name of Jesus Church [6367 St. Charles Avenue, Loyola University campus]. He was the grandfather of young Monroe Labouisse [Jr.] who is following in that same way.[12] I did not win the prize. Bill Gilmer, who was in the class, and I worked together and made measured drawings of the old **Ursuline Convent**.[13] I got terribly interested in that building and the history of it. I guess that was the real beginning of any interest in historic architecture.

The next summer I made a whole sketchbook of sketches — houses, plantation houses — I still have the book.[14] I remember making a watercolor sketch of the **René Beauregard House** in Chalmette [Louisiana], houses on Bayou St. John, the Quarter. By that time, I had gotten to know the Quarter fairly well. That project was for the Churchill Prize. I didn't win the Labouisse Prize, but I did win the Churchill Prize.

When I was in Tulane, Nathaniel Cortlandt Curtis was one of my teachers.[15] He taught me history and theory of architecture. I admired him very much, and he seemed to think I might have some ability. He was with the office of Moise Goldstein. During the summer of my junior year I worked in Mr. Goldstein's office. In those days you considered it a privilege to work in an office like that. You weren't paid anything. It doesn't seem to work that way any more. At the end of the summer Mr. Goldstein gave me a beautiful book on the Tudor homes in England. I'm sure it is something I will have and remember long after I would have remembered the ten dollars a week I might have been paid.

In my senior year, I finished all my design courses by mid semester. I did a thesis. Everyone was terribly interested in Mayan things at that time.[16] Franz Blom was the head of the Middle American Research Institute [at Tulane], and they were sending expeditions to the Yucatán and Central America. I got all hepped up about the Mayas, and I did some kind of a fanciful design for a museum, a Mayan museum. I don't know whatever happened to the thing.

When the Chicago Century of Progress was being planned for 1933, one of the exhibits was to be a reconstruction of the whole Nunnery Quadrangle at Uxmal [Yucatán, Mexico]. There were two architectural students selected to go down and measure the complex, Herndon Fair and Gerhardt Kramer, and Professor Thompson went.[17] If they had taken three students, I was to be the third one, but I missed out on that. I've never gotten to Uxmal. Actually, a Mayan style temple was built in Chicago for the Century of Progress.[18] I went to Chicago for the fair. I took a troop of Boy Scouts. We camped in a beach club on the south side.

Richard Koch — The Historic American Buildings Survey and City Park

Schlesinger: After you graduated, did you have a promise of a job?

Wilson: When I graduated, I spent the summer in Moise Goldstein's office. I started to say, when I got off on the Mayan expedition, I had finished my design course by the end of the first semester. Then I went into Mr. Goldstein's office almost on a full-time basis. I had only one eight o'clock class two or three mornings a week at Tulane. I took the morning off to graduate. Seems to me I went back into the office that afternoon after graduation. It was a horrible bore. Old Dr. Dinwiddie was the president. It was at the Municipal Auditorium. Everybody sat on the stage. It was hot as blazes, no air conditioning.

I stayed on with Moise Goldstein, and of course with Cortlandt Curtis. Their offices at first were in the Hibernia Building. They were building the American Bank Building [200 Carondelet Street, 1928-1929] across the street, next corner. When that was finished, they moved over there. They were also doing the buildings for Dillard University [2601 Gentilly Boulevard, begun in 1930] and Flint Goodrich Hospital [2425 Louisiana Avenue, 1931]. When the hospital was being completed, I had to receive all the furnishings, including surgical instruments, and see that they got into the right places.

Mr. Goldstein was personally interested in the hospital and Dillard University. He was such a close friend of Edgar Stern who was the angel behind these projects.[19]

Nineteen thirty-one was the very bottom of the depression. Things couldn't have been worse. You were just lucky to have any sort of a job. Nothing paid very much, but nothing cost very much either. I could go over to the Holsum Cafeteria and get red beans and rice for lunch for ten or fifteen cents. Things didn't get better. They got worse.

When Roosevelt was elected in 1933, he started the WPA projects, Works Progress Administration, to bring us out of the depression — first was the ERA, the Emergency Relief Administration, then the NRA, the National Recovery Act. There were eagles all over signs. One of the programs that was started was to make measured drawings of historic buildings in the country, the Historic American Buildings Survey [HABS]. It was a joint effort between the National Park Service, and the American Institute of Architects [AIA], and the Library of Congress. The AIA was to furnish the starving architects to make the measured drawings. The rules and procedures were set up by the National Park Service. In fact, it was their idea. It was Charles

Peterson who was then the chief architect for historic structures. He dreamed up the idea and still considers himself the father, and is still fighting tooth and nail to keep the National Park Service from wrecking the thing which has gone on ever since.[20]

Mr. Goldstein, I can't remember if he was the Regional Director of the AIA, but he was at one time. At an AIA meeting he told that the HABS had been set up and each state was to name an architect as the District Officer. He said he would like to nominate Richard Koch.[21] I had met Richard Koch only casually. He had been on the jury that judged one of my senior design projects that won a prize. I went down to his office, and he gave me the prize, a book, and that's all I knew of Richard Koch. Mr. Goldstein said Richard Koch would be ideal to be the District Officer, and I have two men in my office that I'd like to give him. One of them was myself and the other, Monroe Labouisse [Sr.] who had finished Tulane the year after me and came to work in the office when he finished. We went over and started working with Mr. Koch on the HABS.

That's when I really got into doing research on historic buildings. I'd go up to the old **Howard Library** on Lee Circle and read old newspapers. I remember that's how I got interested in Benjamin Latrobe, looking up stuff on the **Louisiana State Bank** building which is now Manheim's [401 Royal Street]. It really had a great influence on my life. In fact, it just set the whole direction.

I used to go out with Mr. Koch. We'd drive all over the state. He was an excellent photographer. We photographed plantation houses. Of course, he had been interested in that sort of thing for years. He had done the restoration of the **Shadows on the Teche** for Weeks Hall and **Oak Alley** for the Stewarts. He had built the Little Theater building [Le Petit Théâtre du Vieux Carré] in the Quarter, renovated **Le Petit Salon**, the Christian Woman's Exchange [**Hermann-Grima House**]. Charles Armstrong (died 1947) was his partner then.

Mr. Koch was also interested in City Park. He was on the City Park Board. He and the Weiss, Dreyfous, and Seiferth office designed the City Park Stadium. In fact, he did most of the design. Then they set up a big WPA project to enlarge City Park.

They took in all the area back of the railroad tracks all the way to Robert E. Lee Boulevard. Mr. Koch was very influential in getting the design of the whole park done by a landscape architect named Bennett. Mr. Koch set up another office in the City Park Casino. Armstrong and Koch had an office at 604 Audubon Building. The Historic American Buildings Survey also had an office in the Audubon Building at 614. When the WPA began working up the big City Park project, a lot of it was done in that office.

I dropped the HABS, except for making trips to the country with Mr. Koch, and spent most of my time on the City Park project. We designed all of the bridges, shelter houses, rose garden, the fence around the stadium. Enrique Alférez did the sculpture.[22]

By that time Charlie Armstrong and Mr. Koch decided to break up their partnership. Dave Geier, who had finished Tulane the year after me, was the chief draftsman for the office in City Park. He went on to work with Charlie Armstrong who became the Supervising Architect for the State Hospital Board when Sam Jones became governor.[23]   Sam Jones was a friend of Mr. Armstrong's. Mr. Armstrong took Dave, and Mr. Koch kept me in his office. Eventually I became a partner.

Schlesinger: You were really into the historical part of architecture from a long way back.

Wilson: Any serious research started with the Historic American Buildings Survey. That's when we found out about the Notarial Archives, the drawings. Boyd Cruise (1909-1988) worked with us. There was no place in the program for an artist, but Boyd needed a job. Boyd and Mr. Koch were friends and both were very active in the Arts and Crafts Club. Mr. Koch thought we ought to have a record of the colors of these buildings. Boyd made hundreds of watercolor paintings of buildings around the countryside and in the city. Mr. Koch had him go to the Notarial Archives and copy drawings in the plan books. Boyd got so intrigued with these records that it changed his whole approach to painting.

The European Experience and the Paris Archives

Schlesinger: What was the attitude toward historic preservation at this time?

Wilson: Historic preservation, there just wasn't such a thing. When I was in school, there was almost a reaction against anything old. Anything that was old was no good. We were on Art Deco, but we didn't call it that, we thought it was modern architecture. Nobody thought about preserving anything. It just wasn't the in thing, even after I went with Mr. Koch.

Colonial Williamsburg had come along [1927] and people began to get interested in that. Things were just beginning then to be oriented to historic architecture. Mr. Koch's work had almost always been in the traditional style with a Louisiana feeling. The first Sunday I was in Paris there was an exhibit in the Museum Jeu de Paume from the Museum of Modern Art. I went in. There was an architectural section. I heard this great booming voice in the next alcove, "Why Richard Koch took that photograph." I ran around, and it was Fiske Kimball who had done a book on American architecture and had borrowed a photograph of one of Mr. Koch's New Orleans [new] houses in traditional style. It was so funny, the first day in Paris to run into Fiske Kimball, who didn't know me from Adam! [24]

I was always very friendly with Moise Goldstein, I stayed very close to him. Mr. Goldstein got me a scholarship with the American Institute of Architects to go to Europe in 1938. That's when I did research in the Paris archives and found out that the **Ursuline Convent** hadn't been built in 1727, not until 1750. The nuns were horrified but they finally accepted it. We had all the documentation, the plans, everything. I found out about a lot of other buildings that had been built in the French Colonial period.

My trip to Europe was quite an event for me. It went on for about six months. This was 1938. The AIA held its national convention here in New Orleans. In connection with the architect's convention Mr. Koch and I and others planned the tours for the visitors. I scheduled my departure after that meeting was over in April.

I sailed from New York on an Anchor liner called *Transylvania*, which subsequently landed on the bottom of the ocean somewhere during World War II. We landed in Glasgow [Scotland]. They were having a big exposition in Glasgow which I enjoyed seeing some of the architecture. I went to Edinburgh [Scotland], Newcastle and York [England]. Then I took a ship to Bergen [Norway] which at that time was great with modern architecture. I took a train to Oslo [Norway] and on to Stockholm [Sweden].

I had the opportunity of meeting Ragnar Ostberg (1866-1945), architect of the Stockholm Townhall which was one of the great buildings of that period. He gave me a book which he autographed. I still have it. I took another ship to Finland.

I went to Helsinki because I was anxious to see some of the work of Eliel Saarinen (1873-1950) who was then living in the United States. He was the hero of modern architects at that time. I went to Göteborg [Sweden] and Copenhagen [Denmark] where the family of a New Orleans engineer, Jens Brae Jensen, lived. He was the engineer who did most of the work for Moise Goldstein's office when I was there. His family took me to their house where they were celebrating his mother's eightieth or ninetieth birthday. It was at that birthday party that I smoked my first cigarette. Everybody smoked cigarettes. It didn't really take.

I made a trip all through Germany. Germany then was under the Nazis. I had to buy my ticket in Copenhagen. I wanted to go to Vienna and Munich, and to Stuttgart where Mr. Koch's family had come from, and on to Paris. I wanted to go to Prague but at that time Czechoslovakia had not fallen to the Nazis. In Denmark they advised me not to go. You could get in, but to get back into Germany to go to Vienna would be difficult. Vienna by that time had been taken over by the Germans. The train into Vienna was full of Nazi soldiers.

I remember walking around Vienna that afternoon and finding the Blue Danube which wasn't very blue. I was walking across the bridge and I noticed that there were crowds of people gathering all along the road and the bridge. All of a sudden this motorcycle caravan came dashing by, big automobile, and everybody, "Heil Hitler!" I stood there with my arms folded. I wasn't about to heil Hitler. They had the townhall all draped with red banners and swastikas. All very dramatic looking.

Schlesinger: Did you have any feeling at that time that there might be a war or not?

Wilson: Yes, everybody thought there might be war, except the Germans you'd meet would say, "Oh, that's ridiculous. We have no idea of war." The Austrians for the most part, they thought it was probably good for Austria. Vienna was a great big city, nothing really to support it. To be tied to Germany would give them a much bigger field of commerce and industry. But the ones who were really suffering were the Jews. There were Judaic signs and yellow stars and all that kind of business going on. It was really a sort of terrifying time.

I guess it was in Nürnberg where they had the Olympics. Finland never got them because the Russians invaded Finland before the war really started. That cancelled the Olympics in Finland. Hitler had built all these stadiums. I think some were in Nürnberg and some in Berlin. They had huge stadiums where they'd have huge Nazi rallies, things we used to see on the newsreels. In Berlin on the Unter der Linden, Hitler had mockup monuments that he was going to build up and down the street. They were just sitting there. In Nürnberg, I think, they were going to build a huge stadium. They had a whole section of it built out of plaster. Hitler was really a frustrated architect.

I finally got to Paris and spent about four months doing research in the Archives Nationales. Everybody was terribly nice to me once I got in. I remember, when I walked into the office of the archivist of the Ministère des Colonies, hanging over his desk was a view of New Orleans in 1726. I almost collapsed. He brought out a box of Louisiana documents, drawings of buildings in New Orleans from the earliest days, maps and all sorts of things.

In France everything closes down in August. The archives closed, Ministère des Colonies, the Archives Nationales, I was working in both places and the Bibliotheque Nationale. I took a train trip around France. Went from one town to the next, got off, looked around, got back on, went to someplace else. Finally ended up in the south of France — Bordeaux, Carcassonne, Marseille, Arles, Avignon.

When I was in Arles things really began to get very touchy about Czechoslovakia. I took the train back to Paris. It was a night train. They came through and pulled the shades down in the coaches at night. It was a black out. When I got to Paris, the street lights were all shaded. When I got to my hotel, there was a pile of sand in the front. Everybody had a pile of sand that you were supposed to throw on the bomb when it came through the roof, almost silly.

It was September, overcast, drizzly rain, miserable. It was the time Chamberlain and Daladier went to Munich and gave away Czechoslovakia and came back with peace in our day. They had a parade down the Champs-Elysées, everybody yelling, "Vive Daladier, Vive Chamberlain." The sun came out and everything was beautiful. Anything would be better than war, and to think of a bomb coming through the dome of the **Invalides** was unthinkable. I guess that's the way most people thought about it at the time.

I had gotten a letter from my brother saying to come home at once, but on an American ship. They just thought that war was going to start any minute. People were lined up at the American Express to get reservations on ships to come home. I had reservations to sail from Liverpool in October. They put on extra ships. People were just fleeing.

Schlesinger: This was nearly a year before the war.

Wilson: It was almost a year. When I got to England, they had mobilized their armed forces. In London everybody went around with a gas mask over their shoulder, terrifying. I took a Canadian Pacific liner home. I landed in Quebec because I was anxious to see some of French Canada.

The European trip was a very important thing in my life because that was where I really found so much that I've used since in my writing and study of early architecture in Louisiana.

Schlesinger: Do you think you are one of the few people who have used these archives?

Wilson: There were a lot of people who have used them, but I don't know of any architectural studies that have been made. In fact, Dr. Waldo Lealand, Head of the American Council of Learned Societies, had worked on the catalog of documents in the Paris archives, *Surrey Catalog,* which I used before I went over there trying to pinpoint things I really wanted to investigate. I went to see him a few years later to see if the council might be interested in publishing. He knew everything in the Paris archives, but he was surprised when I showed him all the drawings.

Schlesinger: I should have phrased my question, I meant, architects from New Orleans?

Wilson: No, I don't think.

Schlesinger: You really pioneered in that study.

Wilson: Yes. The most exciting, when the archives reopened in September, and after the Munich peace — before, if I wanted to have any thing photographed I would have to write a letter saying exactly what I wanted to photograph, kiss your foot letter. I think I had to get a letter from the American consul. When I got back, I went to see the archivist, and he had found another box of Louisiana documents. This was the box that contained the plans of the old **Ursuline Convent** in New Orleans and proved that the present building was not built in 1727 [construction time 1727 to 1734]. There were other things. He said, "Get a photographer here as soon as you can. I wish I could give you these things to take back because we might have a bomb through the roof any day."
I had photographs made. They were all on glass negatives. I still have this box of glass negatives. It weights a ton. I had to drag it home. I had to pay duty on them when I crossed from Canada into the United States because they had been profes-

sionally made. The war started the following September of 1939. We didn't get into it until '41.

Schlesinger: You must have had an excellent knowledge of French to work in the archives.

Wilson: Actually, I didn't. I never did learn to speak French. I had taken French all my life. I took French the three years I was in high school at Warren Easton. When I went to Tulane, French was required in architecture. But none of it was conversational French. I knew how to conjugate a verb but to speak it or understand it, I just didn't at all. I could read the stuff pretty well. In fact, by the time I got finished in Paris I could read eighteenth century French much better than I could read the Paris newspaper.

World War II Years

Schlesinger: When did you become a partner with Mr. Koch?

Wilson: Not until 1955.[25] I had been an associate architect with him. During the war things were pretty slow as far as building was concerned except for defense work. For a while I worked with Mr. Armstrong. Dave Geier and myself set up an office in Pineville, Louisiana and made a study of the central Louisiana hospital there. We lived up there all week and came home for the weekends. I remember having to go through military convoys on the highway. My sister was in the Army Nurse Corps at Camp Claiborne which was near Pineville so I could go visit with her sometimes.

My brother, he was an older brother, had graduated from West Point. When the United States was trying to help the Chinese keep the Japanese out, we shipped things to them over the Burma Road. My brother was out of the army but in the reserve and in the trucking business in New York state. I think it was Franklin Roosevelt and Harry Hopkins who wanted somebody to try and straighten out the traffic on the Burma Road so they asked some of their friends in the trucking business, and they recommended my brother. He was going to go over for the Chinese government until they found out he was an army officer, then put him in the army again. He went over and unfortunately he was killed in Burma [in 1942].

I wanted to get into the service, in the navy. I was very active with my Sea Scouts at this time and didn't want to be in the army. My brother had been killed, that wasn't the reason. My sister was in the army. She had been sent to Australia as soon as we got into the war. I was subject to the draft. They deferred me temporarily after my brother's death.

I tried to get a commission in the navy. I wasn't fat enough. My eyes weren't good. I didn't know my eyes weren't good. I had never worn glasses. The navy doctor said my eyesight was terrible. I did get glasses. I hardly ever wear glasses except to drive, watch TV, a movie, or a play. Otherwise I don't need them. Reading, I do use reading glasses. The navy wouldn't waive eyesight. I ate bananas and drank milk, but I couldn't put on enough weight to make the navy.

I took a course in navigation and took an exam for a commission in the Coast Guard. Some of my Sea Scouts had done that and got into the Coast Guard, but I couldn't pass the physical so I joined the temporary Coast Guard reserve [1942-1945]. One of my brother's best friends was a personnel officer in the Coast Guard, and he arranged for me to go to Gulfport for a couple of months on a pilot boat. We'd go out every night to patrol Ship Island Pass to keep the German submarines from coming in. We didn't have a radio. We didn't have a pistol on board. We didn't have a thing. If the German navy had come steaming in, all we could have done was to wave, and say you can't come in here. Faithfully every night we would be out patrolling the pass. The Coast Guard took over a lot of yachts and put depth charges on some of them. There were submarines out there, and they would drop a depth charge but they weren't fast enough to get out of the way and would almost blow themselves out of the water. They'd come back the next morning with all the caulking cotton streaming out of every seam in the boat. Well, we won the war!

One of the first articles I wrote and had published was in the *United States Naval Institute Proceedings* (Wilson 1944) when I was a sailor in the Coast Guard. I was in the engineering office in New Orleans. The friend of my brother's had me transferred back into the engineering office here where I stayed for the rest of the war, but as an enlisted man. I never got a commission.

Schlesinger: What was your paper about?

Wilson: It was on early aids to navigation.[26] I used to go around inspecting aids to navigation all over the Eighth Naval District. I took my Sea Scouts out sometimes on a cruise and stopped and inspected a lighthouse here, a beacon or buoy there. In fact, gasoline rationing then, they gave us gasoline for our boats.

Before I went into the Coast Guard I worked for a few months with Mr. Koch's brother, Mr. W. E. Koch [an engineer], for the George Glover Company at the Algiers Naval Station. He used to pick me up and we'd go over every morning.[27] One morning when we crossed on the Canal Street ferry, that was before we had the Mississippi River bridge, there were all sorts of ambulances on the ferry.When we got to the Naval Station, ambulances were coming in and there were buses with survivors from a ship that had been torpedoed right in the mouth of the river. I know these things were never in the paper but these people were burned, injured. You really knew that the war was right outside there.

Some Orgins of Wilson's Preservation Philosophy

Schlesinger: Your name is attached to many of our old and new buildings. Would you like to talk about any of them?

Wilson: I've worked with Mr. Koch all those years. When his partnership with Charlie Armstrong ended, he swore he would never have another partner, but he did ask me to be a partner. He had a lot of friends. My interest came from him. Mr. Koch had been in that field long before I even knew him. In the 1920s,

'30s, and '40s we weren't thinking of restoration. We were thinking of saving the old buildings. We now call it "adaptive use"
which was to make them comfortable houses to live in. If the
building required changes, we didn't hesitate to make them. We
never thought about archaeology.
  Mr. Koch made drastic changes to the plan of **Oak Alley**
[plantation house, Vacherie, Louisiana]. It was before my time.
The stairway was in an alcove off the hall. Sort of like the one at
Ashland, now called **Belle Helene**. He did all kinds of things, but
he was very careful to follow all the details of the old house in
things he did. The dormers in the roof at **Oak Alley** were entirely designed by Armstrong and Koch. There were some funny big
dormers in the building before that which may have been later
additions, I never could figure that out.

Schlesinger: Now, in your restoration work, you are a purist?

Wilson: The idea of restoration has changed so much. Again it
depends on what the building is being restored for. **Gallier
House**, at first was bought by the Freemans to live in.[28] So we
remodeled it for them to live in, and they were quite a progressive young couple with interest in modern art. After a few years,
when the little ones became nursery school age, they figured the
Quarter was not the place to live, and so they bought a house up
on State Street. Then the family foundation took over **Gallier
House**. We had to undo all the things we had done for them. Fortunately, we had kept the old service stair and stored it up in the
attic when we took it out and put in an elevator. We had to take
all that out again.[29] By that time, historic archaeology had come
into being, and we had an archaeological study made. The research was done in a much more scientific way.[30]
  At **San Francisco** [plantation house, Reserve, Louisiana]
we did a tremendous lot of research and archaeology before we
even started any work. But as I say, it was not always that way.
There were some buildings we didn't hesitate to remove things
that we thought were not done well. Now, there is a great deal to
do about it, no matter how bad it is, if it's part of the history of the
building everything ought to be preserved. Well, I still don't quite

feel that way. The building ought to be presented in its best form. If somebody has come along and mutilated it, I don't have any sympathy for that. I like to unmutilate it.

Schlesinger: There seems to be a feeling throughout the country of preserving.

Wilson: Yes. In some cases there may be a reason for it. We have been for the last few years working on William Faulkner's house, **Rowan Oak**, in Oxford, Mississippi. There was a nice 1850s Greek Revival house which had been modernized when Faulkner lived there. He did all kinds of things. He built himself a little study on the back of it, a carport, other things. He might have been a great writer, but he wasn't a great architect. Those things were pretty bad. The house is preserved purely as an architectural monument associated with Faulkner and not restored to an earlier period.

Schlesinger: As a shrine.

Wilson: Practically genuflect when you go in. The idea was to restore and preserve it as it was when Faulkner was there. The things that we might consider bad that he did to it have a significance that is not architectural at all, but the association with him. In one of the rooms, Faulkner's office, he wrote the outline of one of his works [*A Fable*, 1954] on the wall. That's all been preserved. In fact, just recently we were cleaning off another wall and found that he had written some more on the walls. We uncovered those writings. I'm not quite sure whether that's the thing to do or not since he covered them up.

Schlesinger: He painted over and you were able to remove that?

Wilson: Yes, we had the archaeologist up there too.

Schlesinger: You have even named an historic district.

Wilson: Yes, the Lower Garden District. Nobody ever looked at that area. I remember one Sunday afternoon Louisiana Landmarks Society decided to have a walking tour of that area with the **Grace King House**[31] and some others. I wrote a little folder that we handed out. We said if we could get a story in the *Dixie* magazine in the Sunday paper that would help. I remember the reporter, "What do you call this area?" I said I don't know, we call it the Coliseum Square Area, but we're also going over to the Annunciation Square. A lot of the architecture looks like the Garden District. "What should we call it?" Maybe we should call it the Lower Garden District. It has kind of a connotation of being a little bit down the social scale as well as in the architecture. And so the reporter thought it was a great idea. It became the Lower Garden District through this article in the *Dixie* magazine.

Schlesinger: I felt that "lower" meant it was closer to Canal Street.

Wilson: It did. It had kind of a double meaning. It was physically below the Garden District. It was at that time almost a slum. When the Friends of the Cabildo did the first volume of the *New Orleans Architecture* series [1971], and called it the *Lower Garden District,* that really started a revival of the area.

Schlesinger: You've had a wonderfully fascinating career.

Wilson: I've enjoyed it. We've had some awfully good people working with us who've been interested in what we've been interested in.

Schlesinger: Thank you, Mr. Wilson.

Notes

1. When Samuel Wilson, Jr. was growing up in the 1920s, the Vieux Carré was in a horrible state of dilapidation — filthy, a haven for beggars, drunks, and toughs. Cheap rents in a European atmosphere of rundown old buildings with wrought iron balconies on narrow streets attracted a group of intellectuals. *Sherwood Anderson & Other Famous Creoles* by William Spratling and William Faulkner is a roster of writers, artists, and architects of the Romantic Renaissance movement.

2. Dorothy G. Schlesinger is the originator of the Friends of the Cabildo Oral History Program. **Part One** is selected parts of conversations she had with Wilson on 9 and 17 July 1980.

3. Wilson's *Impressions Respecting New Orleans by Benjamin Henry Boneval Latrobe,* was a major contribution to the modern interest in Latrobe (1764-1820) who is generally acknowledged as the founder of the professional practice of architecture in the U.S. Latrobe had associations with many important buildings in the U.S. including the **Capitol**. In New Orleans he designed a waterworks, the **U.S. Custom House**, the central tower of **St. Louis Cathedral**, and the **Louisiana State Bank**, now Manheim's. Wilson is a Latrobe scholar, and Latrobe has been a continuing thread throughout his career.

4. Meat, fish, and produce were sold in the old French Market in the Vieux Carré near the river. Although the market place is an ever changing area, and meat and fish stalls no longer exist, fresh produce vendors still conduct business daily. Wilson contributed to the restoration of the French Market complex in 1971. This project won an American Society of Landscape Architects Award, 1976; and an American Institute of Architects Gulf States Award, 1978.

5. Although Henry Howard (1818-1884) designed many public and private buildings in New Orleans and environs, his accomplishments were buried in the historic record until Wilson brought his works to light. In 1952 a photographic exhibit of Howard's architecture was sponsored by Louisiana Landmarks Society to draw public awareness to historic buildings. Wilson selected the buildings to be photographed and the images were made by Clarence John Laughlin (1905-1985) who is now regarded as a major American photographer.

6. Carrollton is located some five or six miles from the center of New Orleans. It was the parish seat, the equivalent to county seat in other states, of Jefferson Parish. Carrollton was annexed to New Orleans in 1874 and is now an integral part of the city.

7. Huey P. Long (1893-1935), governor of Louisiana 1928-1932.

8. Martin Behrman (1864-1925), mayor of New Orleans 1904-1920. Andrew J. McShane (1884-1936), mayor 1920-1925. Behrman was elected in 1925 and died in office that same year.

9. The Tulane School of Architecture was founded in 1907. It was the seventeenth architectural school founded in the U.S.

10. Matilda Stream, heir to the estate of her aunt, Matilda Gray, owns the property at 704 Esplanade Avenue known as the **John Gauche House.** Wilson worked on this building and others in the complex as an associate architect with Richard Koch, 1937-1948. An in-depth historical study was produced by Wilson in 1986 of the five nineteenth century buildings in the Esplanade complex which included the **John Gauche House** plus **Evergreen**, a plantation house in Wallace, Louisiana.

11. **Magnon-Ingram House**, see page 42.

12. Samuel S. Labouisse (1879-1918) was one of the founders of the Tulane School of Architecture. His son, Monroe Labouisse, Sr., was a classmate and longtime friend of Wilson. Monroe Labouisse, Jr. (1940-1986) had won awards for his preservation projects. He had been strongly influenced by Wilson, both as a preservation architect and as a teacher.

13. William C. Gilmer, of Shreveport, Louisiana, designed the Governor's Mansion in Baton Rouge (1001 Baton Rouge Expressway, completed 1963).

14. The 1930 Summer Sketch Book was completed between Wilson's junior and senior years of a four year program. This sketch book, now in the Samuel Wilson, Jr. Papers and Drawings in the Southeastern Architectural Archive, was included in "The History of History in American Schools of Architecture 1865-1975," an exhibit at Columbia University, September 1990.

15. Nathaniel Cortlandt Curtis (1881-1953) came to Tulane from Alabama Polytechnic Institute where he was professor and head of that architectural school from 1907-1912. He was the first full-time architectural educator at Tulane and headed the school from 1912-1917. Curtis left Tulane to take a higher paying job at the University of Illinois but returned to New Orleans in 1920 to take the position of chief designer in Moise Goldstein's (1882-1972) office and to teach at Tulane.

16. The Mayan Revival was the rebirth of ancient American shapes. It was an early expression of a new wave of interest in America's architectural past that took root in the U.S. around the 1920s.

17. J. Herndon Thompson (1892-1969), head of the Tulane School of Architecture 1921-1946.

18. Only the north flank of the monument was built for the fair. It was far from a true reproduction.

19. Edgar Stern (1886-1959) was a New Orleans entrepreneur-philanthropist. Dillard University and Flint Goodrich Hospital were created for blacks (in a segregated New Orleans). Stern was awarded the Times-Picayune Loving Cup in 1930 for his efforts in the establishment of these two institutions. Stern and his wife, Edith Rosenwald Stern (1895-1980), were strong advocates of social justice and used their resources to bring about positive change. (Klein 1984:86-91).

20. Charles Peterson (born 1906) developed his career as a preservation architect with the National Park Service. He has been a dominant voice in the American preservation movement not only through the Historic American Buildings Survey but also through his many publications and his participation in the American Institute of Architects, the Society of Architectural Historians, and the Association For Preservation Technology.

21. Richard Koch (1889-1971) was the first to graduate in the four year architectural course at Tulane University in 1910. He went to the Atelier Bernier in Paris. Koch pioneered the concept of adaptive reuse and the use of eighteenth and nineteenth century Creole forms in his new designs for the Vieux Carré and elsewhere in the region.

22. Enrique Alférez (born 1901 in Mexico), sculptor, has lived and worked in New Orleans for nearly sixty years. His large sculptures decorate major public buildings, parks, and squares throughout the city, and his smaller works are in private collections.

23. Sam Houston Jones (1897-1978), governor of Louisiana 1940-1944.

24. Fiske Kimball (1888-1955) was a recognized authority on historic architecture. He taught architectural history at the University of Michigan and the University of Virginia and was also the director of the Pennsylvania Museum in Philadelphia. He was on the advisory board of Colonial Williamsburg and was involved with the restoration of **Monticello** and **Stratford Hall.** In the 1920s Kimball pioneered investigative research in both his restorations and writings.

25. Richard Koch and Samuel Wilson, Jr. partnership, 1955 to Koch's death in 1971.

26. The essay covered the period 1682-1823 from the first cross erected by La Salle at the mouth of the river to the lighthouse erected at South Pass.

27. Wilson did drafting and supervision on war-related construction.

28. **Gallier House**, 1132 Royal Street, was designed by the noted New Orleans architect, James Gallier, Jr. (1827-1868) for his residence.

29. In 1986 the Ella West Freeman Foundation donated **Gallier House** to Tulane University.

30. Wilson learned about historic archaeology when he visited Williamsburg in 1937, but he did not introduce scientific archaeology, executed by a trained archaeologist, in his projects until the late 1960s or '70s, the time of the **Gallier House Museum.**

31. Grace King (1852-1932) was a noted novelist, historian-writer. Among her better known works is *New Orleans: The Place and the People.*

Part Two

GUIDING CHANGE

Fig. 9. Banque de la Louisiane, 1930.

GUIDING CHANGE

When the idea of preservation first started in the 1930s, there were some who wanted to get Rockefeller to take over the whole thing and restore it like Colonial Williamsburg and make a big museum out of it. That's not what the Quarter is. It is a living thing where people live and work. That's the beauty of it. It is not just a museum.

— Samuel Wilson, Jr.

Historic Preservation Philosophy

Gorin: You are a man with a mission and you have carried out your mission in your architectural practice, in your publications, and in your civic endeavors. This single mission in its broadest term is called "historic preservation."

Wilson: I have been interested in the preservation of buildings and the character of neighborhoods. Every city neighborhood practically has buildings that are not great in themselves but contribute to an ambiance you would like to keep, but you can't keep everything. If everything had been kept a hundred years ago we wouldn't have a lot of things we consider good today. I'm sure there were a lot of people who objected when Madame Pontalba pulled down the whole block of buildings on each side of the public square [Jackson Square] and built the **Pontalba Buildings** but she did it, and I'm sure she didn't have any qualms about it. Now those buildings are among the most important buildings we have in the city.

You have to consider what is going to replace a demolished building. Certainly a parking lot is not a replacement. I think that has to be given a serious consideration when someone applies to demolish a building that has some significance. They should be required to produce some idea of what's to replace it. Also in some cases they'll come up with a development scheme that's great, tear down the buildings, wipe out everything, and then the whole scheme falls through and nothing is ever put in its place. They tore down the **St. Charles Hotel**. They were going to build this great, I don't think it was so great, complex of commercial buildings, but for years it was an open parking lot. The city council can grant permission for a demolition, which they can do, over the recommendations of the Historic District Landmarks Commission or the City Planning Commission or anything else. Those are some of the things we have to think about when we think of preservation, but we do have to keep going, progress!

Gorin: The shape of a city does not happen all at once but over time. Our architectural heritage should integrate with our new architecture, new design. What is saved and what is built should fit together. What are your thoughts about new design in an historic area?

Wilson: New architecture in old areas, I don't think it should be anything exotic, ought to be simple and direct, good proportions, good design. Good design is the important thing.

Gorin: What is good design?

Wilson: That's a matter of taste, and opinion. I don't know how to determine good design. To me, it is something that is pleasing to look at, not disturbing, not intrusive, has good proportions, some good detailing. It doesn't have to have a lot of ornament, that doesn't have anything to do with it. Good design also means it is functional. It does what it is supposed to do.

Gorin: In the name of progress, about 1905 the Vieux Carré lost a square block of Creole buildings facing the 400 block of Royal and the 400 block of Chartres Streets. In this space a new Civil Courts Building was erected. The designers, Brown, Brown, and Marye, were inspired by the then City Beautiful Movement. The building now almost ninety years old is an historic monument, but it is also a monumental example of how not to design in an historic district like the Vieux Carré.

Wilson: There were a lot of people who thought that was the
greatest thing that could happen, just wipe out all those old buildings that were falling down, dirty, unkept. Architecturally, they
were very important buildings. They were part of a grand scheme
developed in the 1830s running Exchange Passage from Canal
Street with a little offset at Iberville, as an approach to the old **St.
Louis Hotel.** [1]

I never looked into it, but I don't think there was any opposition by anybody, maybe Grace King. I don't know how much
she vocally opposed it, but she and her sister went down and
photographed the buildings that were going to be demolished. At
least there is a record of that. Some of the photographs are here
[in the Koch and Wilson office]. They were given to us by Carlton
King, her nephew. Some of them may be at The Historic New
Orleans Collection and at Tulane. Grace King was not a photographer, but her sister, Nina King, apparently was. [2] They took
some photographs in other parts of the city. Grace King was one
of the earliest preservationists around here. She started a group
to try and save the cemeteries, Society for the Preservation of Ancient Tombs. [3] It was the beginning of preservation around here.

The Courthouse [**Civil Courts Building**, 1906] is a big
building of white marble, terra cotta, completely out of scale with
anything in the neighborhood. I remember when I was in school,
Professor Curtis told us about an article he read in the *Journal of
the American Institute of Architects*, entitled "Speaking of Ugli-
ness." That building was the subject of that article. It was not
good design. It has too many things going on. The marble and
the terra cotta have changed colors at a different rate. The building is just completely out of place. I don't think it was ever good
design.

In some of Nina King's pictures, when the site was cleared,
you can see the old **St. Louis Hotel.** There were very few people
who were trying to preserve anything. Professor Curtis was very
interested in the **St. Louis Hotel.** He wrote articles about it, made
drawings of it. He studied the construction of the dome which he
considered a very innovative method of tile pot construction. The
dome was still visible. He salvaged a few of the pots and had them
up at the Tulane School of Architecture. When they tore the

building down, he got some of the capitals of the great Corinthian columns of the rotunda, the Ionic columns from some other part. We used to sketch them in freehand drawing class. Whatever happened to those I don't know. They were huge, great scale. I don't know what happened to the clay pots. They are probably around town somewhere.

Professor Curtis made suggestions to convert the **St. Louis Hotel** into a convention center which was an early presentation of that sort of idea in New Orleans. His efforts weren't very effective. It would have been a disaster. The only thing that would have really been worth preserving was the rotunda, which was the thing Professor Curtis was intrigued with. He thought in order to save the rotunda they would have had to do something [politically favorable] like a convention center. It would have involved tearing down another block of very important early nineteenth century buildings, the **Seignouret House** and all the other houses from the hotel site back to Toulouse Street, some were very important. It would have been great to have preserved the rotunda, but not at the expense of all those other buildings.

Royal Orleans Hotel

Gorin: Change is inevitable and new architecture is bound to be built. The architect has a significant role to play in the critical issue of guiding urban change in a sensitive and orderly manner. During the era of the post World War II building boom, you were a significant player in guiding change not only in the Vieux Carré and the Central Business District but in other sections of our city as well. One of your keys to guiding change has been the design of new forms based on historic models. Perhaps your finest hour in this regard was your contribution to the designs of the Royal Orleans Hotel in the late 1950s.[4]

Wilson: Richard Koch and I were working together, and he contributed a lot. These are all not my designs in any way.

Mr. Koch was a fairly good friend of Edgar Stern. Mr. Stern had bought the site of the old **St. Louis Hotel**. He had Mr.

Koch draw a set of plans from the records in the Notarial Archives of the old **St. Louis Hotel** [in 1946]. These plans were not working drawings but an historical study.[5] I don't know if Mr. Stern had some vague idea in the back of his mind that he'd like to rebuild the old **St. Louis Hotel**, but it was not in any way a practical thing to do.

[In the 1950s Edgar Stern selected the newly formed firm of Curtis and Davis, a modernist team, to design a new hotel for the historic space that the **St. Louis Hotel** had formerly occupied.] In the beginning we had nothing to do with it. They had the building designed as to the structure, room arrangements, bathrooms, all that goes into the hotel. Since the building had to be approved by the Vieux Carré Commission, we were to come up with a design that would meet the requirements of the Commission.

There was a fragment of de Pouilly's building still standing on Chartres Street. There was some idea at first that they would take that down and stick it on the wall in a courtyard. I thought it would be nice to leave that fragment there and extend it with the necessary alterations in the spacing of the arches all around the ground floor of the new hotel. We took down the de Pouilly granite arcade, marked every piece, put a new foundation under it, put it back exactly where it was, and continued it from there in stucco cement to form the rest. We worked on designs and sketches and came up with what the hotel finally ended up with.

Gorin: Was it ever considered to recreate the dome of the old St. Louis Hotel in the new structure and in the manner of de Pouilly's clay pot construction?

Wilson: No, it certainly wouldn't have been a practical thing to do. The dome of the old **St. Louis Hotel** is a very interesting thing. The hotel was begun in 1835 by de Pouilly. Apparently, there had been a competition to select the architect and the de Pouilly brothers won. They worked in kind of a French way. I think they were influenced by the buildings on the Rue de Rivoli in Paris. They wanted to have a big rotunda on the interior, but it was not an element of the exterior. Gallier,[6] who was doing the **St. Char-**

les Hotel at the same time, had the great dome on the outside and that was a very conspicuous feature of the building, but it was an inconspicuous element in the St. Louis Hotel exterior plan and an important element in the interior of the building.[7]

De Pouilly built the St. Louis dome out of wood, big wood ribs and plaster. A few years after the building was completed, it caught fire and burned and the wooden dome was burned and destroyed. When they rebuilt it, following pretty much the same plan that they had done originally, they decided to try to make the dome fireproof. They developed a clay pot — looked like a flower pot, closed in at both ends with a hole in the center of each end, slightly tapered. They built them up like hollow structural clay tile. It reduced the weight of the dome, real vault, real dome, structural masonry. With Latrobe's dome, the building that is now Manheim's, the old Louisiana State Bank [401 Royal Street], he did that in brick. The masonry is much heavier than the light weight dome that de Pouilly did for the St. Louis Hotel.

When we got into the workings of the Royal Orleans, the structural design had already been created. We couldn't change any of the column spacing or anything else. We did design the interior, the lobbies, the Rib Room, the ball rooms, the public spaces downstairs. We did the garage elevations, the pool deck on the top. All the details were done in our office. I would say that I had a lot to do with those elements.

Gorin: An imposing view of the Vieux Carré, the river, and parts of the city can be seen from the pool deck of the Royal Orleans Hotel. It is not just the view that makes this area a special place, but it's your subliminal use of historic forms in your design, your choice and arrangement of elements in human scale. You have created a sense of place, and even though the environment has all the amenities of modern luxury, there is historical continuity. The dominant element in your scheme is an arch. What was your model?

Wilson: It was based on the Thierry House, 721 Governor Nicholls Street, which Henry Latrobe[8] and Lacarrier Latour designed and built for Jean Baptiste Thierry, who was the editor of the *Louisiana Courier,* newspaper. The house had been built in 1814. It had an open gallery that had been closed in. When we did the repairs, turned it into apartments for Miss Sarah Henderson in 1940, we took the stucco off the front and you could see the columns and the arches. The columns were there with the moldings still intact where they closed them in. Miss Henderson said let's go ahead and restore it. That's how that came about.

The façade had Greek doric columns with segmental arches which I'm sure were designed by Henry Latrobe. Lacarrier Latour probably did the back of the house with a great big arch and two little cabinets in typical New Orleans French Creole style. We used that façade in developing the pool deck at the Royal Orleans.

Later on, the hotel owners wanted to enlarge the building. We went back to see what Mr. de Pouilly had done, and he had a mansard roof with a balustrade around the top. We put that roof on to increase the room capacity of the hotel. From the beginning, we had to get height variations from the Vieux Carré Commission to do that. There was some opposition to it. I felt the building that had been there originally, which was one of the most important buildings in that part of the city at that time, was that height. The Courthouse across the street [**Civil Courts Building**] was that height and did bother a lot of people. I argued in favor of the variation. We were trying to maintain the mass and a little bit of the feeling of the old **St. Louis Hotel**. Generally, the people in the Quarter agreed that it was an asset. It had been a junk yard for years. They tore down the old **St. Louis Hotel** in 1916. It had been a lumberyard, all kinds of junkie stuff there, a fence around it. I remember banana trees hanging over the fence.

Gorin: How did height limitation come about in the first place?

Wilson: Arbitrarily, was it in Paris in the days of Napoleon III they arbitrarily said no building can be over fifty feet high? All the buildings in Paris were that way until recent years. In the Quarter, just an arbitrary number. Don't think there was any average of building heights. I don't think the Royal Orleans exceeded the limit by a terribly large amount. I'm not sure about the **Pontalba Buildings**.

I think it's fine to have a limit like that, but I think some variations are OK depending on the location, the surroundings. Even a fifty feet height in an area where everything is twenty-five feet is not good. It ought to have some relationship to the surrounding area.

Board of Trade Plaza

Gorin: Your Board of Trade Plaza, a small urban park, won an AIA award in 1969, and a New Orleans Chamber of Commerce award in 1973. This project, located at 310-320 Magazine Street, was not an historic district in 1966, and did not become an historic district until 1978, yet you sensitively designed new architecture to continue the scale and personality of the surrounding urban fabric. Or as post-modernist Robert A. M. Stern might say, you found a reusable past.

Wilson: There was an old building that had been built as a hotel by L. E. Reynolds, the architect, about 1860. The building was a four or five story building, brick masonry, lots of cast iron. The ground floor had cast iron columns and arches. The windows had big cast iron lintels and decorative elements. The building was in very bad condition. It settled unevenly. The Board of Trade's main building was in the back on Board of Trade Place, a little alley that runs through there. To get to that building you went through the old hotel. They decided it was time to demolish that building before it fell. They interviewed several architects as to what they would do with the land. I suggested that they save some of the elements of the old hotel and create an arcade that would form an entrance into the Board of Trade Building. Use some of them as decorative elements on the opposite wall. They seemed to like that idea so they gave us the job.

Mr. Koch designed the fountain in the center. He loved those octagonal fountains that he had seen in Spain and Mexico. There was one in the courtyard of the Little Theater [616 St. Peter Street] he did long before I was with him. Billy Burkenroad happened to be traveling in Spain or Italy, and he saw this cast iron fountain. He was on the building committee of the Board of Trade. He bought the fountain. He sent us a picture and wrote to us; would this be appropriate? It was exactly what we wanted. That's how the fountain got in the middle of the plaza. The fountain was to be there, but we didn't know where we were going to get it.

All the cast iron elements were salvageable. The building was taken down very carefully. All the pieces of cast iron were taken out toward the lakefront, can't remember where, stripped off all the old paint, and painted with yellow rust inhibitor paint. We have slides of all those pieces sitting around a building yard waiting to be reerected in the plaza.

Anglo-American Art Museum

Gorin: There is another outstanding project in your catalog that demonstrates your talent for designing something new out of something old. I'm referring to the Anglo-American Art Museum in Memorial Tower on the Louisiana State University campus in Baton Rouge that opened in 1962. You designed the historic galleries. How did you get that project, and how did you find the authentic materials to construct those rooms?

Wilson: An anonymous donor wanted to establish a museum that would show the influence of the English on American art and architecture. I was on the board of the state museum at the time, and we got a letter from the anonymous donor's attorney asking if we were interested in accepting a sizeable donation, and what could we do?

We could work a museum into one of the buildings that we had, but we were also interested in the French, Spanish, and other influences in Louisiana. LSU said they would give two big rooms in Memorial Tower. It was decided to accept the LSU offer. John Canaday was the art advisor to the donor. He said I should be the architect for the museum that was going to be created.

It was going to be mostly a portrait gallery. The donor had

some real funny ideas that these had to be pure Anglo-Saxon types, and they had to be approved by, I think, the Smithsonian Institution anthropologist. Had a little racial overtone, I thought. They were going to have copies made of portraits in England and British Museums. John Canaday was supposed to go and select the paintings to be copied. The head of the art department at LSU, Bosch, said she wouldn't have anything to do with a museum that was going to be a bunch of copies. I said you don't have to have copies, you can get good originals in this country. At that time you could buy Thomas Sully (1783-1872), Gilbert Stuart (1755-1828), Benjamin West (1738-1820) — good artists at a price that was within the budget of the project, and you could probably get good British portraits, maybe not the top artists but good. They decided to go that way.

Before they came to that decision, Dr. Bosch wanted to give the money back. Dr. Borth, who was the comptroller at LSU, had already received the grant, invested it, and just about doubled it while all this was going on and wasn't about to give it up. That's how we finally decided to go out and buy American things. The art teachers said can't we do some architectural backgrounds for these portraits of various periods? Why not get some rooms?

I remembered seeing some rooms on Camp Street, I used to walk down Camp Street on the way to the office, that had some beautiful Greek Revival details. These rooms were in an automobile windshield replacement place. Their motto was "Don't Cuss See Gus" so I went to see Gus. They said we could have the plaster cornices, plaster rosettes, door trim, and the carvings. That was one of them.

I went to New York and found a little Philadelphia room at Ginsberg and Levy. Later I went with Dr. Borth and Dr. Bosch up to New York to see if we could get some English rooms. French and Company had an English room that was quite good, very expensive and beyond the budget. We did find a doorway we bought, but we didn't know what we were going to do about the main rooms.

When we got back to New Orleans, Sis Ochsner, Dr. Alton Ochsner, Sr.'s [of Alton Ochsner Medical Foundation] daughter, called. Could she come by, she had something that maybe we could help her with. Some Texan had donated an English panelled room to the hospital. They didn't have any use for it. Did we know anybody who'd be interested in buying it. I said that is exactly what we've been looking for. It was in a warehouse on Baronne Street. It was a beautiful room. Not only that, there was also a Jacobean Room. We got them from the hospital for much less than things we had looked at in New York. That is how we put those together.

    We wanted a similar room that would represent the American things. Mr. Koch and I remembered a house outside Woodville, Mississippi that was practically a ruin that we had been through twenty-five years before. We managed to find it again. The house was stored with hay. Someone had ripped off one of the boards of the mantel, looking for buried treasure or something. We found the owners. There were five heirs, one was in Japan, one in Maryland, others goodness knows here. We were finally able to get them all together, and they agreed to sell it to the University. We took the whole room out piece by piece, floor boards, ceiling boards, wood work, everything. We managed to reconstruct it exactly the same size. I think we moved one door a foot or two to one side. I forgot why, but it worked out fine.

Hermann-Grima House

Gorin: Even the finest of old buildings can outlive their usefulness. This was the case of the Hermann-Grima House at 820 St. Louis Street, a mansion with kitchen and stable buildings all substantially in the same form as they were built. You guided change at a significant time in the history of this complex of buildings when you helped the owner, the Christian Woman's Exchange, redefine its purpose for owning the property.

Wilson: It is one of the most important buildings, I think, in the Quarter. It is a pretty important architectural example built in 1831 by an American builder, William Brand, who had come down to Louisiana and was in business by 1805. He'd done a lot

Fig. 10. Hermann-Grima House, 1930.

of work on other buildings. He did this house for Samuel Hermann.

   The Christian Woman's Exchange bought it in 1924. They were interested in helping working women, primarily, to give them a little shop where they could sell their handwork and also to provide rooms where working women could live for a reasonable rent if they were employed in department stores on Canal Street. Armstrong and Koch did a lot of renovations to the building when the Exchange bought it. They added dormers on the back of the roof so they could use the attic for rooms, renovated the rear wing. In fact, we did the renovation of the rear wing a couple of times. I handled most of that myself. We've never found any original plans, drawings. We've found building contracts from 1831. Very seldom that you find any drawings for these early buildings.

   Eventually the Christian Woman's Exchange realized that the building was not being used to the full idea they had of helping working women. Working women by the 1960s didn't need that kind of help, they were quite self-sufficient. So they said, "What do we do with this beautiful building?" I said, "Why don't you restore it as a historic house museum."[9] They all seemed to take to that idea. In fact, they made me an honorary Christian Woman in 1971.

We began the gradual restoration of the building as an historic house museum. I remember when we told them the woodwork, which had been painted white for many years, was originally wood-grained. They couldn't understand what wood-graining was all about. They thought it was an awful idea. We got John Geiser [III], who was still in business at that time, to come down and help us.[10] He scraped down some of the doors, and they saw what the graining was. He refinished one of them. Then they realized that this was the 1830s, and it was not painted all white. Now the wood-graining and marbling of the base boards are their pride and joy. They love it.

Restoration of the kitchen was a long drawn out process. It started out [in 1966] with Mrs. John Manard, now Mrs. Truman Woodward, John died some years ago, everybody calls her "Shingo." She was very active in the Exchange. We started by figuring out what the kitchen was. She did a tremendous lot of research on kitchens of that period. She traveled around the country. Henry Krotzer [architect, then with Koch and Wilson] got involved; he'd worked on the kitchen at **Gallier House**. Of course these are different period kitchens. We scraped down walls, found where soot marks were that indicated where ovens were and other equipment of the kitchen. The chimneys and the flues were all still there. I think we made as authentic a kitchen that could be just from evidence, not from actual remains, because there was very little left except the big open fireplace in the main kitchen.[11]

Gradually over the years they've done more and more in the restoration. They first did the ground floor [of the mansion]. They've been working on the upper floor. They did want to use the upper floor for meetings of the organization and some entertaining that they do. We had to make changes to conform to the fire laws — put up exit signs, put in a sprinkler system, emergency lighting which is not terribly attractive, but it had to be done if they were going to use the upper floor. We try to make them as inconspicuous as possible but they definitely have to be seen.

Same with smoke alarms stuck upon the ceiling. We've gotten used to seeing these things. People are not as conscious of them as you might think they would be. They are accepted in today's living.

We haven't provided handicap access to the building. I don't know if we ever will. Probably could be done without too much difficulty. There's no elevator.

Magnon-Ingram House

Gorin: You are a functionalist, a pragmatic man. You are much more concerned about making a wall safe and sound than saving the patina. When you consider the technology that has become commonplace in your lifetime — such as air conditioning, central heat, swimming pools, elevators, burglar alarms, plastic materials, the list is long — by our standards, you make a building better than it was to begin with. The art in your architecture is the bringing together of the old and the new but always retaining the historic ambiance. The Magnon-Ingram House, 620 Ursulines Street, and The Historic New Orleans Collection, 527 Royal Street, are extraordinary examples of modern conveniences in an historic setting. The Magnon-Ingram House was a million dollar job. Did you have carte blanche?

Wilson: I wouldn't say that. When Fritz Ingram bought the house, his decorator was Vera Duvernay Gibbons, a friend of mine. It was she who recommended me to Fritz Ingram. They eventually got another decorator; in fact, they went through two or three decorators before the house was finished. Then, they did it over again. I had nothing to do with that. When we did it, Fritz Ingram said he didn't want any publication of the house at all. He wanted it done very quietly. When Valerian Rybar, a big New York decorator, I had worked with him on other jobs, did it over, I understand they spent another million dollars. At that time it came out in *Architectural Digest,* a beautiful set of pictures and write up (Carlsen 1980).

The work that we did was a million dollars. That was a

whole restoration of the building. We had to do a lot of structural repairs; we built some new buildings in the courtyard, swimming pool; we added a guest wing, a lot of stuff besides just the house.

We rebuilt the chimneys because they wanted to use the fire places. Those old chimneys are usually a dangerous thing. The bricks crack and fire can start in attics. We had to rebuild the chimneys and put in flue linings. The walls were all in pretty good condition.

Gorin: Did you have any termite damage?

Wilson: Termites were not a problem in that particular house as I recall. Termites are always a problem, have to protect against them, but I don't remember any serious structural damage from termites.

Gorin: Did you have to put in any tie rods to brace the walls?

Wilson: We put some in later when we noticed movement in the walls. I did a lot of research on the background of the house. It was originally a two-story house that had been done by the architect-builders Gurlie and Guillot [Claude Gurlie and Joseph Guillot] in 1819 for a man by the name of Arnaud Magnon. He was a ship builder during the Spanish period. He built ships that were used in Galvez's expedition against Pensacola, I believe. He had a little shipyard at the river and Ursulines Street. In 1818 the city decided that shipyards were not an appropriate use of the riverfront. It should be for the people. It should be a park. We hear all this today. The city bought Magnon's shipyard. I think he was eighty-five years old at the time. So he used the money to build the two-story house, had Gurlie and Guillot do it.

In the main room upstairs, the front room on the lakeside[12], it still has the cornice they designed with carved swags which became a trade mark of Gurlie and Guillot. They used it in cornices all over the city. They built a whole bunch of buildings in the 1830s that has this swag, a garland — the **Tricou-Wogan House** at 711 Bourbon Street, the **Gally House** at 536-542

Chartres Street. Magnon's house, I guess, was the first example of it. It was all still there.

The top story was added in the 1830s. The cupola was added then. Rooms on the ground floor, originally just store rooms, were where the shipbuilder had moved his equipment from his shop when they demolished it. It was remodeled in the 1830s by Madame Poeyfarre in the Greek Revival style.

Gorin: Did you begin this project with measured drawings?

Wilson: Yes, we had to go down and make measured drawings of it which we still have. In fact, we made measured drawings modeled on the Historic American Buildings Survey. I've never given them to the Library of Congress [repository for HABS documents]. Fritz Ingram at the time had some misgivings at letting the plan of his house made available. He was always afraid of robbery. If fact, they were robbed at one point. He no longer owns it; other people are living in it. I will probably donate these drawings to the Library of Congress.

We do the historical research at the same time we do the drawings. You have to remember this was a house that a family was going to live in. So we had to work toward their needs. We had to take some areas and put in modern bathrooms. Mrs. Ingram wanted a nice dressing room and closets for a large wardrobe. We did have to make concessions. We did not do paint archaeology. That was before we got into the paint archaeology business.

Gorin: Did you do any archaeological digging on the grounds?

Wilson: No, all that came later. The idea was to do the house really better than it had been. We replaced the cornice. Whether the original cornice was like it is now, we don't know. We had no very early photographs. We based it on other buildings of that type. The little attic windows still had the fine cast iron grills in the windows. We developed a new wood cornice because none of that was there.

Gorin: When you installed the swimming pool, did you have any problems with nearby buildings from taking too much moisture out of the ground?

Wilson: The Ingram house had a big courtyard area. I don't know of any effect on surrounding buildings. We haven't done too many pools in the Quarter. We did one for the Streams on Esplanade Avenue. They had a big side yard, and it didn't effect anything as far as I know.

One of the worst things was when the Royal Sonesta Hotel was built, and they put a two story parking garage under it. When that was excavated all the buildings around it began to crack. That was a terrible problem. We were not involved with that part of the design of the hotel, fortunately. There were lawsuits. Pounding the sheet piling, seepage. It did drain the water out of the ground under the surrounding buildings. It wasn't until the building was completed that the surrounding buildings could be repaired. I don't think we lost any buildings, but it certainly was a serious thing. I certainly wouldn't advocate underground parking in the Vieux Carré.[13]

The Historic New Orleans Collection

Gorin: The Magnon-Ingram House is a private building whereas the Historic New Orleans Collection is a public building and can be enjoyed by everyone. Stewart Farnet, past president of the New Orleans chapter of the AIA, said that The Historic New Orleans Collection is his favorite among your work. He also said that he goes out of his way often to enjoy the strength and grace of that really wonderful work and with each passing he finds new delight in its use of materials and the easy relationship of its parts. He called it an original and creative work (Farnet 1986).

Wilson: It is five different buildings all interconnected.[14] It's not easy to do that. We've had to do all kinds of things to make some of them accessible. A lot of changes had to be made.

During the lifetime of General and Mrs. Williams, they lived in the residence that Mr. Koch really restored for them [718 Toulouse Street].[15] Someone climbed over the wall one night and frightened Mrs. Williams. After that she was afraid to live down there, so they bought the house up on Coliseum Street. We did some work on that for them. They lived there until they died.

They had moved all the furniture out of the [Vieux Carré] house. They had photographs made of it. In their wills they wanted the house restored as they had lived in it, so we had to rerestore it as a house museum. The **Merieult House**, 527 Royal Street, the ground floor had been a series of shops. We restored one as a library and one as the exhibition room that they would have open to the public every day, and a gift shop. We did these things in various phases. The gift shop expanded from one area to another. The library expanded. We put an elevator in. We had to find a place to put that without destroying anything.[16]

The air conditioning went in various phases. I'm sure the Williams had air conditioning in the house when they lived in it. I don't remember too much of those details.

The Williams owned the building at 722 Toulouse Street which was quite an early building. There is a drawing of it in the Notarial Archives made in the 1850s, and it shows what it looked like. We tried to get General Williams to restore that too. He partially restored the rear on to the courtyard, but it wasn't until after the Collection was really going that they decided to restore it on the basis of the early drawing. We did it over as the archive building for the Collection.

There's a building at 714 Toulouse Street that the General had sold to Clay Shaw years ago.[17] He liked Clay Shaw, and he thought he was doing great at restoring old buildings in the Quarter. So he sold it to him, and the Collection had to buy it back. We restored that. Main thing, when they bought the building back, they needed a connection from the Royal Street buildings to 714 Toulouse so we devised a bridge across a patio at the second floor level that tied them together. There is no direct connection to the building at 722 Toulouse which is the Archives and Manuscript Collection. You have to go through a patio. All other buildings can be reached through doors one way or another.

We restored the exterior and adapted the interior of 714 Toulouse for the curatorial section — storage space for materials, file cabinets, and reading room which they named for Richard Koch. They call it the Richard Koch Reading Room which I thought was a nice gesture. They would like to be able to expand even more because they keep getting more and more materials. The Collection keeps growing. They did buy some warehouses on Tchoupitoulas Street which we restored. They had hoped that they would be rented in part to produce revenue. Some of it would be used for their offices and conservation laboratories, air conditioned temperature control storage vaults. They haven't used it entirely as they had intended. I think they still have expectations of doing it. With the rental market as it is they have not been able to produce any revenue out of the building.

Gorin: How would you appraise Clay Shaw's restorations?

Wilson: He saved the buildings. I don't know how well they were done. I never thought they were really top quality restorations. At least he saved the buildings and made them useful. I think he contributed a lot in that way.

Gorin: The Collection, meaning the library and the archives, was built on the Williams private collection. Fire protection of these rare books, documents, and art work was no doubt a high priority.

Wilson: Although the buildings themselves are great architecture and historically significant, the collections they house are just as important, if not more so. We recommended a Halon system. This was the thing for the preservation of historic documents and other valuables that could be destroyed by water. The Halon system is devised in which a gas is released to smother the fire without damaging the contents of the building. We didn't want to have those things damaged by a sprinkler system. Water damage from sprinkler systems, which had been in use before, sometimes had done more damage to collections than the fire. I think they have a monitoring system. Fortunately we've never had to use it.

Gorin: The Koch and Wilson additions, new designs which reflect the nuances of the nineteenth century New Orleans architects' vocabulary, are so well carried out by expert craftsmen that I am unable to distinguish between what is old and what is new. What was the Koch and Wilson philosophy on the issue of distinguishing the reproductions from the originals?

Wilson: There was a lot of fuss about you should make it obvious, what was new and what was old, but we didn't feel that way about it. We thought it all should look alike.

Orue-Pontalba House

Gorin: In the decades of the 1950s and 1960s the New Orleans preservation community had one crises after another, and wherever there was trouble you always seemed to be there. Le Petit Théâtre du Vieux Carré's demolition of the Orue-Pontalba House, a late eighteenth century building on the corner of Chartres and St. Peter Streets, was a very controversial issue in the early 1960s. Now with some distance of twenty-five years or so, was demolition the right course of action?

Wilson: I think it was. The building was in very bad structural shape. I imagine it could have been saved if the owners really had wanted to, but they wanted to make it into something else.[18] With the structural condition as it was, they were given permission [by the Vieux Carré Commission] to demolish it.[19]

The building has been altered through the years. It was a very old building. It was started right after the fire of 1788, and it burned in the fire of 1794. We found building contracts for it. It had been started by a Spanish official, José de Orue, who was a Spanish treasurer, or something, of the colony. He sold the building to Almonester.[20] Orue had contracted with Hilario Boutté, a general contractor, to rebuild it after the fire. Orue was going to have the iron work made by Marcellino Hernandez who was a Spanish iron worker from the Canary Islands and was probably the best craftsman of the Spanish period in Louisiana. Before Almonester finished this work, he sold the building to the Baron Pontalba with the agreement that he would finish except Almonester wanted to build a less expensive balcony than one by Marcellino Hernandez. There was a lawsuit over it.[21] We have all of this in the court record which is great to have. Almonester was compelled to complete the balcony as he'd agreed. Hernandez also did the iron work on the **Cabildo.**

When we rebuilt the building, we reused the iron work. The balcony had been altered. It had been extended out over the whole sidewalk. When we rebuilt it, we put it back the way it obviously had been originally, a three foot balcony. There had been other changes. The building originally had a flat terrace roof. The theater wanted some attic space so we did a roof, but concealed it more or less behind a balustrade which was reconstructed.

I sort of withdrew from the project. Mr. Koch handled it and Henry Krotzer. I didn't agree with some of the things that the Little Theater people wanted to do. I dropped the whole thing. On the uptown end of the building there was what obviously had been a little side yard which had been closed in. As I remember it, they wanted to change the façade to include this extra ten or twelve feet on the end which I thought should not have been done. They wanted to raise the ceiling height and some other things I didn't agree with.

Gorin: I sense that you are not willing to concede the over all mass and proportions of a building like the Royal Orleans Hotel and this theater building. You want those precise.

Wilson: The Royal Orleans does not, except in its general mass, relate to the original **St. Louis Hotel** because it has more stories, doesn't have the high ceilings that the 1830s building had.

Gorin: I'm referring to the over all mass of the building, height, width.

Wilson: Yes.

Gorin: Did you reuse the bricks from the old building?

Wilson: I don't think very many were reused.[22] We used the doors and windows and all the millwork that was useable and the ironwork. We were able to reconstruct the building more like it had looked when it was originally built.

Gorin: But you said earlier that you rarely find old plans and drawings. How do you form a conjectural model when you have no hard evidence?

Wilson: You try to think what would they have done at that time. Studying other works of the same architect, the same period, see what was the general way of doing things. You may find that your decision was not correct when evidence is uncovered later on. That has happened extensively in Colonial Williamsburg. They've found a lot of things they did in the beginning were not correct. They've had to do them over again. They continuously research to make things as authentic as possible but there is no way to be perfect about it. Colonial Williamsburg has the money to go back and change things which we seldom do around here.
        We think the **Orue-Pontalba House** was designed by Gilberto Guillemard who did the **Cabildo**. We had some drawings he had done for a house for Dr. Montegut's daughter at 731 Royal Street. It showed the way he did the balustrade around the top and the corners. We used that in some of the reconstruction of the lower floor which had been so completely altered and the balustrade around the top. There were changes in the façade — quoins in the center pedimental bay had been removed on the ground floor. I'm sure they were there originally so when we redid the building, we added them on the ground floor [then they corresponded with the existing quoins in the center pedimental bay, second floor].

Gorin: After twenty-five plus years, the reconstructed Orue-Pontalba House, up to the time it was recently painted, had the patina of its historic neighbors and looked like it had been there for a hundred years. Are we fooling the public?

Wilson: Certainly not intentionally. There's a bronze plaque on the building that says it's a reconstruction from the 1960s. It's reproducing essentially the building that was there as it was originally designed. The plaque on the **Orue-Pontalba House** was placed there by the Orleans Parish Landmarks Commission.

Gorin: How did the Orleans Parish Landmarks Commission come about?

Wilson: It had been established by an act of the legislature in 1956 largely through the efforts of Leonard Huber and John J. Petre who was the representative from New Orleans in the state legislature at the time.[23] When John Petre was running for the senate, one of his platforms was to have the important buildings in his district marked with bronze plaques. Leonard saw it in the newspaper and said if you're going to do it in the sixth and seventh wards, it ought to be done citywide. I think Leonard was president of Landmarks [Society] at the time. He went up to Baton Rouge and talked to some of the legislators and with the help of then Senator Petre and State Representative Lucien T. Vivien, Jr., the bill was passed and the Commission was created.

    I was appointed to that commission and have served on it. Leonard was the president and after his death, I became the president. Over the years we have placed over a 100 bronze plaques on buildings around the city. People stop and read the plaques. The important thing is to have the information as accurate as possible. We used to get an appropriation from the state but they cut that out years ago. I don't think the state knows we exist any more.

Fort St. Jean Baptiste

Gorin: Following the Orue-Pontalba quasi-reconstruction, in 1963 you did preliminary studies for a replication of Fort St. Jean Baptiste in Natchitoches, Louisiana and, in 1979, the actual construction of the colonial fort.

Wilson: The idea of rebuilding Fort Natchitoches goes back a number of years. There was Mrs. Irma Sompayrac Willard from Natchitoches who was terribly interested in this project some years before I was involved in it. She had a model made, got a lot of publicity, and had a lot of people interested. Eventually, they were able to get the state legislature to appropriate funds to do it.

When I did research in Paris [1938], I found Broutin's original plan after he had made a trip to Natchitoches in 1732. We took that plan and had a large scale print made, an eight scale in American measure. The dimensions were all in French. We used that as a plan. As to what the buildings looked like depended on what we had seen in other early buildings of that period and what we had seen in the Paris archives.

A lot of work of this sort had been done in Quebec. The great fort at Louisburg, it was a French bastion in Canada. It had been restored. We were in contact with those people. We visited a number of fort replicas. We went over to Jacksonville, Florida where there is a replica, supposedly, of the first French fort, 1660s. It was done for the National Park Service. I thought it was pretty bad. It had concrete blocks in the structure. It was two-thirds the size of the original, not on the original site. It was in a beautiful location. They had a fine reception center and museum, but the fort itself I thought was pretty bad.

I went to the fort at Jamestown in Virginia, went to Mackinac in Michigan which was a very good replica. I had met the architect and was in correspondence with him, got some of his plans to see how he went about that. I think his name was Dick Frank. I went to Harrodsburg, Kentucky, which I had visited years before, which was an early replica from, I think, the 1920s. I later made a trip to Pennsylvania, Fort Ligonier. It was an American revolutionary fort. It was a very good replica. We got a lot of ideas from those visits and studying the manuscripts of the period of the fort. We tried to make it as authentic as possible.

Gorin: How did you convert the old French unit of measure on Broutin's plan to our standard of measure?

Wilson: They had what they called French feet which was slightly larger than an English foot. Some surveyor worked out a table so you could translate French feet to English feet without any trouble.

James Pitot House[24]

Gorin: Another aspect of your preservation work, and Mr. Koch's too, is to move houses and then restore them.[25] You moved one house by floating it on a barge down a bayou. Another house you cut in three sections and moved it that way to a new location. A small 1830s cottage with a side gallery was rolled into the 1984 Louisiana World Exposition for an exhibit. You've moved a total of five buildings, among them the Pitot House. This late eighteenth century Louisiana plantation house of the French West Indian type is a house museum as well as the home of the Louisiana Landmarks Society. How did you go about moving this one?

Wilson: First we had to figure out how to move the columns intact. They were old bricks plastered over. We got some heavy timbers and set them vertically around the columns and tied them in, like putting splints on a broken arm. We managed to save most of them without breaking them. The walls, we tried to save some of the bricks to use in the rebuilt walls. We got a lot of volunteer help from the bricklayers. We used brick and concrete blocks. We didn't attempt to reproduce the original materials in the reconstruction of the ground floor except for the columns which are the most visible element of the building.

We moved the columns away, took the walls down. We did have to shore up the galleries on the second floor. Then we were able to remove the brick work of the ground floor. Lowered it and put it on a truck and moved to the new site [about a block away]. Jacked it up and the columns were put back. The important thing was the salvaging of the columns by putting heavy timbers around them and taking them down in one piece.

A wing had been added on the back. We took it off before we moved the building. When we took the siding off the back of the house, on the second floor we found the original turned

columns sealed in the walls. We filled in between the columns
with louvers copied from the **Whitney Plantation**.

Gorin: What was the preservation philosophy that guided the res-
toration of the Pitot House?

Fig. 11. Pitot House, 1930.

Wilson: We were not thinking about James Pitot or anybody
else's time. It just seemed that early nineteenth century was the
time that the house was designed. Actually, it may not have been.
As we examined the house and saw the construction, we realized
that was the form. When we found the Charles Alexandre Le
Sueur sketch from France, it confirmed our ideas and so we restored it to that point. It was that way for the first half the
nineteenth century. I thought it was a nice way to do it.

Gorin: How did you find the Le Sueur sketch?

Wilson: There were a couple of articles published on Le Sueur, 200 sketches of New Orleans. Leonard Huber went to the museum in Le Havre and had a lot of the sketches photographed and brought them back. That sketch was among those.

Gorin: How much of the house did you change in the restoration?

Wilson: The main thing is in the shape of the roof. It was then a single slope. In the construction, the trusses, the roof framing, it was typical French colonial style — main truss members framed on the main walls and at a lesser pitch over the galleries outside. In the 1850s, or maybe later, they were having trouble with the roof leaking with the break in the pitch. They jacked the outside rafters up, just lifted them up off the trusses, and extended them so they came up out above the old ridge. We could see the nails and pegs where the rafters were originally. We took the extensions off the rafters, dropped them back, and they fell into place in the roof form as it was originally. The only problem, the workmen who lowered the roof didn't secure the outer ends, the nails were loose. When Hurricane Betsy hit [1965], the wind got under the roof and lifted the whole thing off — all original rafters, all original construction. We salvaged them and put them all back when we rebuilt after the hurricane.

Gorin: Was it a jigsaw puzzle to reconstruct?

Wilson: No, it was so obvious. We removed the old screening and the railing on the gallery. The replacement railing we modeled after the Le Sueur sketch, and also we took from the comments of C. C. Robin who came up the Bayou around 1800. C. C. Robin wrote an account of his visit to America, and he said the houses along the bayou, some of them were in the Chinese taste. We assumed he thought this was sort of a Chinese Chippendale railing. There were probably other houses that had the same thing. We didn't hesitate to put the railing back that way.
    We began to think that maybe the end gallery was a later addition. There may have been gable ends to the house but we never got into that. We were pretty well satisfied with the results.

The restoration was based on hard evidence of the build-ing, sketches from Le Sueur, journals from Robin and the knowledge we had of the architecture of that period.

Gorin: Digging out and interpreting the historic written and graphic records, synthetizing that information with what you find in the fabric of a building, then translating it into three dimensional form in correct scale is a special talent of yours that separates you from most architects and from your critics. The historian-writer Charles L. "Pie" Dufour said that you are unparalleled in New Orleans re-search; and very few people have the historical depth, perception, and appreciation of what they know as does Sam Wilson (Gorin 1986a).

Notes

1. The **St. Louis Hotel** was designed by J. N. B. de Pouilly and occupied the site, St. Louis, Royal and Chartres Streets, from 1835-1916.

2. Some Nina King photographs are in the Gargoyle Society Collection, Southeastern Architectural Archive.

3. About 1923 the Society for the Preservation of Ancient Tombs was organized. Grace King was honorary president. The society reported a membership of over 150. They began a research project to determine the location and condition of the tombs of greatest historical significance and then undertook efforts to have them restored (Wilson 1974:ix).

4. The Royal Orleans Hotel and the Royal Sonesta Hotel are the two largest projects in Wilson's catalog. Both hotels are models of how to guide change through the use of forms with an historic memory to fit into the total design system of the historic district.

5. Wilson did the historical research and supervised the restoration drawings. A drawing of the **St. Louis Hotel**, pencil sketch on paper with color pencil addition, 10-3/4 x 21-3/4 in., is in The Historic New Orleans Collection. It is inscribed Richard Koch, Architect, New Orleans, 8 September 1949, but is the work of Wilson.

6. James Gallier, Sr. (1789-1866) was one of the most successful architects of New Orleans in the mid-nineteenth century. Gallier and his partner Charles B. Dakin (1811-1839) designed the **St. Charles Hotel**, the **Merchants Exchange**, the **Arcade Baths, Christ Church**, and several fine houses. When James Dakin (1806-1852) joined his brother, Gallier withdrew from the partnership to practice on his own as both architect and builder of residential and commercial commissions. Gallier completed **St. Patrick's Church**, 1839-1849, after Dakin and Dakin withdrew from the project. Among his last and best known works was the classic **City Hall**, 1845-1850, which, after the construction of a new city hall in the 1950s, was called **Gallier Hall** in his honor (Wilson 1982:153-154).

7. The first **St. Charles Hotel**, 1835-1837, 200 block St. Charles Avenue, designed by Gallier and Dakin, was the American rival to the Creole **St. Louis Hotel**. The first **St. Charles Hotel** burned in 1851 and was rebuilt without the dome to plans by Isaiah Rogers; modified by George Purves. In 1894 the **St. Charles** burned and a new one was designed by Thomas Sully, opened in 1896. The structure that was demolished in 1974 was the third **St. Charles Hotel** on this site. In its place now stands the Place St. Charles, a high-rise office building.

8. In 1812 Henry Sellon Boneval Latrobe (1792-1820), son of Benjamin Latrobe and also an architect, came to New Orleans to construct his father's waterworks. He also erected the building for **Charity Hospital**, elegant houses, the building for Davis' ballroom, designed and built **Christ Church**, Episcopal, and prepared a design for the lighthouse at the mouth of the Mississippi (Wilson 1951:xxii). Henry was stricken with yellow fever and died on 3 September 1817. The elder Latrobe came to New Orleans to complete his waterworks. He too was stricken with yellow fever and died three years later to the day, 3 September 1820, after his son's death. Both father and son were buried in St. Louis Cemetery No. 1, but their grave sites have been lost. Descendants of the architects have erected a plaque in the Protestant section to honor them.

9. By the 1960s there were hundreds of house museums in the country, but in New Orleans the idea was a novelty. Of the eight historic house museums in the city, Wilson has been involved with the restoration of five of them: **Beauregard-Keyes House, Gallier House, Hermann-Grima House, Williams Residence** (in The Historic New Orleans Collection complex), all in the Vieux Carré, and **Pitot House** on Bayou St. John.

10. John Geiser Inc. was a painting and decorating service. At this time the company was owned and operated by John Geiser, Jr. and John Geiser III; they offered graining, marbleizing and other types of traditional painted decorative work.

11. In 1973 and 1974 archaeologist J. Richard Shenkel, professor at the University of New Orleans, supervised a student who conducted archaeology in the kitchen. In 1975 Dr. Shenkel conducted a major excavation. The kitchen has been rerestored based on archaeological evidence.

12. Reference points or directions in New Orleans are given in terms of Lake Pontchartrain, "lakeside" or northward; "the river," the Mississippi, or southward. "Down-river" means an easterly direction and "up river" is westward.

13. This problem did not exist with the Royal Orleans Hotel because the building was depressed into the ground only a half floor below grade.

14. The Historic New Orleans Collection Museum/Research Center consists of the **Merieult House**, 527 Royal Street, the Counting House in the rear of the **Merieult House**, and townhouses at 714, 718, and 722 Toulouse Street. The **Merieult House** is one of the oldest buildings in the Quarter and the only building in this area to survive the great fire of 1794.

15. In 1938 General L. Kemper (1887-1971) and Leila Moore (1901-1966) Williams purchased a parcel of four buildings at the suggestion of Richard Koch. The Williams, collectors of rare Louisiana textual and graphic materials and art works, endowed The Historic New Orleans Collection which opened in 1970.

16. When designing new equipment in old buildings, elevators for example, the problem of retaining aesthetics is compounded by Vieux Carré Commission regulations and building codes. The Historic New Orleans Collection elevator was designed to rise in the attic and not on the roof, as anything effecting the exterior of a building is subject to approval by the Commission. In the case of the **Miltenberger House,** Dumaine and Royal Streets, Wilson ran the elevator up the back of the building and screened it. Early elevator installations in stair-wells, such as Wilson found in the **Pontalba Buildings,** no longer meet fire codes.

17. Clay Shaw (1913-1974) was a businessman associated with International House, International Trade Mart, and the French Market Corp. He was active in historic preservation and restored nine buildings (*The Times-Picayune* 1976).

18. Le Petit Théâtre had outgrown its facility and wanted a new building with new spatial arrangements.

19. Before issuing the demolition permit, the Vieux Carré Commission re-quired a signed bonded contract and letter from the legal representatives of Le Petit Théâtre stating that after demolition, the reconstruction of the theater would begin.

20. Don Andres Almonester y Roxas (1725-1798) was the Spanish grandee who provided funds for rebuilding **St. Louis Cathedral** after the great fire of 1788 and who built the **Cabildo,** 1795, and the **Presbytere,** ca. 1791-1813 — all of which flank the north side of Jackson Square. He was the father of Baroness Pontalba who built the **Pontalba Buildings** which flank the east and west sides of Jackson Square. Father and daughter, with their wealth and desires, shaped the appearance of the heart of the old city.

21. Lawsuits are one of Wilson's favorite sources of information on a building's history.

22. The bad structural condition was proven in the demolition process as all but about a thousand of the old Louisiana red bricks turned to powder.

23. Leonard V. Huber (1903-1984), second president of Louisiana Landmarks Society, 1956-1958, was in the business of cemeteries and in the design and con-struction of monuments and mausoleums. Huber published on a number of subjects such as cemeteries and monuments, architecture, and steamships. Among his books are *New Orleans: A Pictorial History; Louisiana: A Pictorial History;* and *Landmarks of New Orleans,* a compilation of buildings designated with plaques by the Orleans Parish Landmarks Commission, introduction by Wilson.

24. James Pitot (1761-1831), mayor of New Orleans 1804-1805.

25. In 1922 Armstrong and Koch took down the old **Hurst Residence**, a plantation type house, 1832, up river from the Vieux Carré near Tchoupitoulas Street and Nashville Avenue, and reerected it on a suburban site. The architects used measured drawings of the building made by Tulane students. Examples of these drawings are in the *Tulane Department of Architecture Yearbook, 1913-1914*.

Part Three

AN AMERICAN ARCHITECT, AN AMERICAN PLACE

Fig. 12. Beauregard House, 1930.

AN AMERICAN ARCHITECT,
AN AMERICAN PLACE

Practically from its beginnings in 1907 the Tulane
University School of Architecture encouraged the study and recording of
Louisiana's historic architecture. Tulane students continue to produce
measured drawings of old buildings and architectural details, as well as historical studies, for which the S. S. Labouisse Prize is awarded annually.
                                                        — Samuel Wilson, Jr.

Cabildo

*Gorin: Historical time is connected by man-made things, architec-
ture being among man-made things. There are three important
buildings in our city — three distinct shapes in time — that represent
three different periods of political domination. The Ursuline Convent was built during the French regime; the Cabildo built during
Spanish control; and St. Patrick's Church is symbolic of New Orleans as a young, growing American city. These buildings are in
reality dialects between generations of designers, builders,
craftsmen, and expressions of technological developments. You,
Mr. Wilson, have brought to these buildings your knowledge and the
technology of your time to continue life in these three man-made
monuments. The Cabildo, because of its role in American history,
is the most prestigious building that you have worked on, twice now
— the 1966 rehabilitation and the current reconstruction after the
1988 fire. Your studies of the Cabildo began as a student, then as a
member of the HABS team in the 1930s. Let's talk about some of
the research you have done to portray historical time in three dimensional form.*

Wilson: The **Cabildo**[1] has had all sorts of things done to it over
the years. When it was first built, it was constructed over the
remains of the old French *Corps de Garde*, the police station,
which had been built in 1750. It burned in the fire of 1788. The
walls stood. It was cleaned up and a new roof was put on. It was

used as a temporary church while the **St. Louis Cathedral** was being rebuilt after the 1788 fire.

Doing research we found that they again reused those walls when the new Cabildo was being built [1795-1799]. They had to get permission from the King of Spain because the *Corps de Garde* was a royal establishment belonging to the king. The king was delighted because they could build the city hall above it, and he wouldn't have to worry about the leaky roof. The city would have to worry about that on the building they would construct over it.

I looked into the French *Corps de Garde*. When the building was turned into a museum in 1911, they knocked out one of a series of five arches down the middle of the *Corps de Garde*. We did archaeology [ourselves] and found that the foundation of the middle pier had not been knocked out when they put a great big arch there so they could have a bigger museum space. We rebuilt that arch on the foundation that was there.

We dug down and found the brick floor that was the floor of the *Corps de Garde*. The floor is just as it was described in the records of 1750 — bricks on the flat, bricks on the edge. There were fireplaces, one on each side, on the far ends of the building. Windows were apparently like the windows of the old **Ursuline Convent** which was built at the same time by the same architect, Bernard Deverges, after Ignace François Broutin died in 1751. Deverges took over all the work. We copied the windows of the **Ursuline Convent** and put them in the St. Peter Street side of the building. Those windows had determined the location of the windows in the *Sala Capitular* on the second floor.

We tried to restore the *Sala Capitular,* which is one of the most important rooms in American history, where the transfer of Louisiana to the United States was signed in 1803. It had been ripped out to make a great big room for the Louisiana Supreme Court and the front wall of the building was knocked out to make a gallery part of the courtroom. They did all kinds of strange things. We tried to restore it as far as possible like the rooms were when the building was constructed.

The room downstairs on the side nearest the church, we found was the lamplighters' room where they kept their oil and what-not that they used when they went out at night to light the street lamps. It had a fireplace; evidence was on the blackened walls. We found floor tiles; we put in a new floor that was like the old one. We tried to keep it like the character of the old room as much as possible.

Upstairs were the Mayor's parlor and the Mayor's office. They had all been ripped out as part of the museum, or maybe part of the court. We put those back. All that was lost when the Sun King exhibit was installed [1984]. When they got rid of that, the museum personnel put it all back, but they did not make any attempt to rerestore what we had restored.

The lower run of the main stair in the **Cabildo** has treads of marble which are very badly worn. They are not used except on rare occasions. In other words, they are not open for general use. We put another stairway in the back of the building. There's a stairway on each side used on ordinary occasions, and there's an elevator we put in the back. The worn out marble is sort of history of the building. Martha Robinson said she'd murder me if I took up those worn marble steps that all those great people of the past had walked on.[2] Also, the stucco on the outside has been patched and patched over the years. It's in very bad condition, and a lot of the masonry underneath has deteriorated. Now I think they are working on that. We are not involved. To do a restoration of an old building, it does lose a certain charm of antiquity. It is very nice to see the plaster falling off but that's not going to save the building.

Gorin: Where did you find records of the Cabildo?

Wilson: I found some in Paris. I found most of them in the Library of Congress. It was probably when I was working on the Latrobe Impressions, late 1940s. I went to the Manuscript Division. They had a box of miscellaneous Louisiana manuscripts. Garland Taylor was the librarian at the Tulane Library. I told him about this; he got interested. The Library of Congress got interested and numbered and cataloged every document. Before, all I could refer to was a box of documents. It is all microfilmed and up at the Tulane Library. The Library of Congress had bought the box of documents in North Carolina. The librarian said it had been on the shelf since 1911, the year I was born, and nobody had ever looked at it.

Here were all the records of the engineers and a list of the people Pauger had made when he granted lots in the original city around 1722. It was amazing what was in there — records by the engineer Broutin of the **Ursuline Convent**, *Corps de Garde*, all these buildings that the French had built. They made what they called *toise de batiment*, a quantity survey. That's the way they paid for the building — the number of cubic yards of excavation, cubic yards of masonry, board feet of lumber, pounds of iron, squares of roofing. All were listed. I learned a lot about the **Ursuline Convent** that I hadn't found in Paris in 1938.

The most important thing was the list of the people who had been granted lots in the original city. They were all numbered. I thought that there must be a map to go with this. I went to the map division, looked through the card file and found a "Plan of New Orleans, 1803." Wondered what that is? They brought it out, and it was the map that the list was the key to.

The same thing had happened in Paris. I found a beautiful map of Gonichon's of 1731. When I got home and was going through my notes from the archives, here was the list that corresponded to the numbers on that map. So we had the list of property owners of 1731.

Archivists, librarians — if it's a manuscript it goes in the manuscript division, if it's a plan it goes in the map division. They may be twenty miles apart. There's no coordination.

Gorin: After sixty years of historical building research experience, what are your words of wisdom about this tedious job?

Wilson: Lot of it is a lot of luck! You get a hint that something might exist somewhere and you follow it up. Sometimes you hit pay dirt. Sniff it out like a bird dog. We are fortunate here in New Orleans to have the Notarial Archives which is a relic of the French and Spanish periods. I didn't read French very well when I went to do this research, but I read it enough, fifty-four volumes of correspondence in the National Archives in Paris dating from

1698, 1699 to 1803, page after page, scanned, made notes. I have ten little notebooks full of transcripts from the archives. I should have done a little more research, I would have found that they all had been transcribed before and were in the Library of Congress. I could have done all this research in Washington instead of Paris but it wouldn't have been nearly as much fun.

Gorin: According to a retrospective lecture of the Cabildo's 1960s rehabilitation that you gave to Friends of the Cabildo in 1984, you discussed two important design decisions: one, that the oldest part of the building, the French Corps de Garde, was restored to its approximate appearance at the time it was completed in 1750; and two, the rooms on the second floor were restored to their approximate appearance at the time of the Louisiana Transfer in 1803.

Wilson: I worked closely with Peggy Richards, who was then the director of the museum. It was pretty much agreed to restore the second floor as much as possible to the period of the time of the Louisiana Purchase. I think that is the attitude of the Museum Board today [reconstruction after the 1988 fire], but there are a few things the museum wants to do. One of the things I didn't agree with was when we did the work in the 1960s, we found that the *Corps de Garde* on the ground floor still had the brick floor that was laid in 1750 when it was the old *Corps de Garde*. We exposed it, barricaded it off so you could walk around it, look into it, but not walk on it. When they had the Sun King exhibit during the world's fair [Louisiana World Exposition, 1984], they put a temporary wood floor over it. The floor is in much worse condition than when we finished with it in the '60s. The museum said let's cover it up and put the new floor level with the other floor because the old floor is about twelve to fifteen inches below the level of the surrounding rooms. We are going to put a new brick floor over the whole thing and leave a small area only of the original floor exposed. I didn't approve of it. The director [James F. Sefcik] was insistent on it.

Gorin: To leave a unique aspect of a building's construction visible is one of your basic tenets of historic preservation. You left a sag-

ging wide beamed board ceiling in view in the library at The Historic
New Orleans Collection and also an iron thistle style ventilator in
the wall in the Counting House there.

Wilson: I would prefer to leave the floor like we had it before.
This means that you have to build something over it. That didn't
have anything to do with the [recent] fire.

Gorin: How did the fire of 11 May 1988 get started?

Wilson: The fire was apparently started from a torch of a
workman who was soldering or working on the gutters as part of
an exterior renovation that was underway at that time. Evidently the fire got under the slates of the roof and smoldered probably for quite some time before it was discovered. Fire Chief
McCrossen has gone into it quite extensively and that seems to
be his opinion.[3] Probably there are some claims against the contractor for the damage that was caused.

Gorin: Have you ever had anything like that to happen on one of
your projects?

Wilson: No, fortunately not, but it can happen. You are not supposed to use open flames or anything like that. Or if you do,
they're supposed to have a fire extinguisher right there to control
anything like that but evidently that wasn't done.

Gorin: Did the building have a sprinkler system?

Wilson: The building did not have a sprinkler system. When the
building was renovated by the WPA in the 1930s, the idea of a
sprinkler system was apparently accepted as the right thing to do
in museums. As time went on the idea among museum people
changed, and they felt that a sprinkler system would do more
damage than the fire. When we did the renovations in the 1960s,
it was decided to remove that old sprinkler system, which was
probably pretty much deteriorated. So there was no sprinkler system in the building. There was a fire alarm system, and I under-

stand it functioned properly. Now things have changed again, especially after the fire. The sprinkler system is acceptable in museums, and we are going to put in a new system.

Gorin: Before the damage was cleaned away and the second floor covered, there was a good view of the charred remains of the cupola and third floor of the Cabildo from the pool deck of the Royal Orleans Hotel. What internal damage was there to the rest of the building?

Wilson: All the plaster was damaged by water. The building was unroofed for a number of months before we could even get a temporary roof put on it. There was no way to put anything on it with the remains of the structure there. It all had to be cleared off down to the level of the floor. Anything that you would put over it would cup and just collect water that would be more damaging than rain. Don't think the damage from the rain was anything compared to the water that was put on to extinguish the fire. The fire did not go below the third floor, fortunately.

Gorin: Was there any damage to the pediment?

Wilson: We're not sure how much can be attributed to the fire and to the work that had to be done to take the damaged materials off the roof.
    We checked all the walls of the building. We found the front wall, the pediment, leans eleven inches out of plumb. We found some evidence of cracks opening between the front wall and the cross walls. This must have been going on for years. We found a report from an engineer in 1955 that the wall leaned at that time nine inches out of plumb. Over thirty years or more, it increased. Some of the movement in the outside walls was the result of the fire. Changing the roof load stirred things up. It was finally decided that the walls had to be tied together with tie rods so we ran tie rods crisscross through the whole building. That was quite an undertaking. They've all been put in. We've tried to conceal them as much as possible. You can't see them from the outside but you can see some in the ceiling of the arcade on the

ground floor. There'll be one or two that will be visible in some of the rooms on the second floor.

Gorin: These new tie rods are now part of the history of the Cabildo, and the fact that they show only ties into your principle of leaving in plain view unique construction techniques of the time. In the Koch and Wilson reconstruction drawings will there be any redesigning of interior spaces?

Wilson: Only on the third floor. The basic structure is going to be reproduced just as it was, the big timbers and all that. The museum wanted to make a few changes in the arrangement. Mechanical equipment in the attic space above the third floor, the museum had found it difficult to maintain the equipment properly in the cramped space so we took an area on the third floor and moved the mechanical equipment there.

Gorin: It sounds like some of the work you are doing now needed to be done and the fire had nothing to do with it.

Wilson: Yes, that's true.

Gorin: There are fire code requirements to be met since the 1960s project. It's possible, new fire codes may come out of the 1988 fire.

Wilson: That's another one of the problems we have. When we did the work in '65 we added an elevator and a stairway in the back which was not damaged by the fire. They're still in perfectly good condition. From the third floor, the two exits would be the new rear stair we put in the '60s and the main stair. Now the fire code doesn't allow the main stair to be considered as an exit because it is open at each floor, enclosed at the third floor. They want us to enclose it at either the second floor or the first floor. At the other side of the building there is another stair that went up from the ground floor to the second floor. They want us to extend that up to the third floor.

Gorin: Disasters — hurricanes, earthquakes, and in this case, fire

*— can serve as a catalyst for architectural research. Since this dis-
aster, what direction has your historic research taken?*

Wilson: I've been doing a lot of research in the records of the
City Council and the Mayor's Messages. We're finding a lot of
details of when the Supreme Court went into the building. We
found that over the years there have been so many changes on the
inside. The wall between the *Sala Capitular* and the room next
to it was removed, and we haven't been able to determine exactly when that happened. I'm still trying to find out something
about that. About 1869 they knocked out the front wall between
the *Sala Capitular* and the room next to it, the gallery. They
knocked the whole wall out and put in a couple of columns. They
later put the wall back. The cast iron columns are what they put
in when they took the wall out between the *Sala Capitular* and the
room next to it. Two columns in the front wall they evidently put
in 1869. That opened up the whole end of the room to the gallery. Later they closed it up again. You can still see these
columns in some of the old photos.

There's a question now about the location of the fireplace
in the *Sala Capitular*. We found evidence, in the way the floor
was framed around it, that the fireplace was on the long wall. The
director [Sefcik] thinks maybe it was at the far end, above the
fireplace in the *Corps de Garde* and under the fireplace on the
third floor. We found no evidence that there was anything like
the evidence of the location we picked to restore the fireplace on
the second floor.

*Gorin: Would you be more specific about the evidence you found
in the floor?*

Wilson: The way the floor was framed, a joist had to be cut off to
support the hearth and the chimney. I think the director thinks
that was done when they remodeled the place for Lafayette.[4]
We found the plans Guillemard made in 1799 for a prison
building that was in back of the *Corps de Garde* on the ground
floor. Unfortunately, he doesn't show what was on the second
floor. In 1833 Joseph Pilié made a series of drawings to remodel

the building which were all not carried out, some of them were. Latrobe made a little sketch from memory from visits to the place. We're convinced the fireplaces are in the proper place.

Gorin: After the 1988 fire, Koch and Wilson Architects was selected over eleven Louisiana architectural firms who applied to restore the Cabildo. William R. Brockway, chairman of the State of Louisiana Architect Selection Board, said that you know more about the Cabildo than any other person in the world. In your body of knowledge about this building are the HABS drawings that you worked on almost sixty years ago.

Wilson: Charles Peterson [founder of the HABS] thought it was a great opportunity to record the important buildings of this country in measured drawings that could be used in case of a disaster. Certainly in the restoration of the **Cabildo** those drawings were very helpful. They saved us a lot of work, and they showed us what changes had been made over the years. We used them to arrive at what we thought was the best way to restore the building. In Europe after the destruction of Warsaw and other cities during World War II, it was measured drawings that had been made before the war that enabled the reconstruction of them. When we were in Warsaw, it was amazing how well it was done. It was all due to the foresight of recording historic buildings in the form of measured drawings.

Ursuline Convent

Gorin: Disasters are probably our first associations with the value of the HABS concept, but as a practitioner, this pool of information is part of your standard research resources.

Wilson: The drawings that we made in the '30s for the **Ursuline Convent** were used when we made the model [of the complex restored, 1966] and thought we were going to restore the whole thing.[5] It gave us knowledge of the roof construction, roof framing, roof form, and the details of the dormers.

Gorin: The Ursuline Convent is another building that you probably know more about than anyone else. Your research began as a student, then the HABS. Your published research in 1946, the equivalent of a master's thesis, was the first systematic scholarly inquiry into the history of any building in New Orleans. As a practicing architect, you contributed to the restoration of the old Gate House in 1942. What work was done at that time?

Wilson: The Gate House was included in the HABS measured drawings. The work we did, as I recall, was not part of the overall restoration that the archdiocese was going to undertake, but something Father Liberto, the pastor, wanted to have done because the Archbishop had allowed him to open it to the public. He wanted to have a little museum in that building which the Landmarks Society arranged for him.

We had to rebuild the roof. I don't know when the roof was changed, but it had a very awkward roof, low pitched, sticking-out rafter ends that didn't belong with that building. We redesigned the roof from old photographs that showed little finials on the corners of the ridge.

When they wanted to lay out the garden in front, I made a sketch for it. I remember going to see Mayor Maestri[6] about it with one of the ladies [Ursuline Auxiliary]. The city may have contributed, I don't remember.[7]

Gorin: Is the garden that exists today your design?

Wilson: Yes. It is based on the design of the early French botanical garden which was across Ursuline Street. It shows on some 1730s plans. I just took that and adapted it to the size of the property.

Gorin: Your 1966 restoration of the roof and the dormers was the beginning of what you thought was going to be a total restoration?

Wilson: It actually turned out to be that way, but I didn't have anything to do with it after the roof and the dormers.

Gorin: What work was involved in the dormers?

Wilson: Many of them had been changed over the years; only two or three looked alike. Actually, when the building was constructed there was no sash in the windows, just shutters. The intent of the restoration was to give all the dormers the same appearance, and as the original drawings indicated — to restore

Fig. 13. Ursuline Convent, 1930.

the sides with wood parallel to the roof and to add wooden shutters. There were never any plans. The original drawings and possibly the original dormers seem to have been built with a masonry front. Big, heavy dormers on Broutin's drawings and described in the *toise de batiment* that we found. Apparently, it fell to pieces in an early stage and wood fronts were put on them, and that's what we restored. We didn't attempt to restore the original masonry; we had so little evidence what that was. They [Archdiocese] did not agree to the wood siding or shutters. I think the shutters were a financial question. Now the shutters are on but I didn't have anything to do with it. I think they did use our drawings from back then.

Gorin: In 1970 you were consulted on saving the eighteenth century walls of the chapel Almonester had built for the nuns. The New Orleans States-Item (14 May 1970:29) carried a story about the demolition of the St. Mary's Italian School building behind the Convent and the restoration of the chapel walls. There was a picture of you and Father Liberto in the story.

Wilson: The chapel had been built in 1787. In the 1870s the archdiocese wanted to have a seminary so they added two stories above the chapel — took the roof off, laid a floor, used those walls, and built up two stories which later became St. Mary's Italian School. When the school closed [1963], it was decided that the building was not in sound shape, really condemned. It was to be torn down. When they started opening up the walls, we could see the Spanish arches and some of the hinge pins still in the walls. They were obviously the walls of the Almonester chapel.

The archdiocese agreed to retain those walls. They put a temporary roof over the first story walls. I had several ideas what to do. I thought it would be nice to restore the chapel, and that's the way it was shown in the model. I also thought, if they couldn't do that, to preserve the walls and lay out a garden. They would become garden walls. Nothing was ever done about it, the walls deteriorated, and they finally tore them down.

Gorin: Why didn't you get anymore work at the Ursuline Convent?

Wilson: At the time we put a new slate roof on the building and restored the dormers the contractor had to take off the old slates and, of course, a lot of dust filtered down into the attic. The ladies, the Ursuline Auxiliary, would take tours through the building for fifty cents a head. They were annoyed that the dust came down on them. They should not have been up there in the first place. The contractor also had to replace some of the timbers, mostly sheathing, the wood deck to nail the roof to, and in doing that, he had to remove some of the wiring that they used to light up some of the trusses and beams which were the most interesting things of the attic tour. The Ursuline Auxiliary got very annoyed at me. They said I was never down there. I was down there more than on the usual jobs. There was not that much I could do. As if I could tell the contractor that he couldn't drop dust on the ladies' heads. There was no way you could do that and do the job.

Gorin: How were you informed that you wouldn't be doing any more work on the Convent?

Wilson: I didn't hear anything about it. There was a Christmas Eve party at John Geiser's [III]. Father Nicholas Tanaskovic, who was the pastor of the Cathedral, was there. "I'm sorry that you're not doing the convent. They've got another architect."

St. Patrick's Church

Gorin: St. Patrick's Church, the corner stone laid in 1838, is the most important example of Gothic Revival architecture in New Orleans. Its massive tower, equal to eighteen stories, was for many years the tallest structure in the city. Your relationship with St. Patrick's Church is much shorter than the Cabildo or the Ursuline Convent, only about thirty years. How did you get started with St. Patrick's?

Wilson: When Betty and I were first married, we lived in the Quarter at 620 Governor Nicholls Street.[8]
   At first, we went to church at **St. Mary's** which was around the corner from where we lived. Father Gagliardoni was the pastor, and he spoke with such a heavy Italian accent Betty said she couldn't understand a word he was saying. Next Sunday we went to the Cathedral. Father Thomas spoke in French. We struggled

through that for sometime. When we heard that **St. Patrick's** had been air conditioned, we went to **St. Patrick's.**[9]

Father Bezou was the pastor, and we got to be friendly with him. Father Bezou was the one who got me started doing architectural work for the church, like when the liturgy changed after the second Vatican Council in 1965, I put new altars in the front. He wanted me to design the new front altar, which I did, and which is still in use. He wanted me to do a lectern which is still in use. I did some work on the entrance doors.

When Father Bezou was transferred, Father Reynolds wanted me to continue. We got into a big project for a real restoration of the building starting with the roof. We put a new roof covering, went over all the structural work under the building, termites had attacked. We are just about to finish it.

The main trouble, the building was stuccoed with a pebble dash, awful stucco that was popular in the 1910s and 1920s. It doesn't really adhere to the walls and sometimes pops off. We would have loved to take it all off. For many years the church was just brick. It would cost a fortune to take off the old stucco which would also take off some of the brick surfaces. That's something that's in abeyance. It continues to fall even though we've had to replace a lot of it.

The major work has been replastering the interior. The great vaulted ceiling is all plaster with plaster ribs. They were falling and could be very dangerous — great hunks of plaster fell right down on the pews, which were never occupied. We had to scaffold the whole church, go through every bit of the plaster to see that it was secure. We replaced a great percentage of it and found the wood frame underneath it in many cases was completely rotted out from leakage. All that had to be replaced.

We've worked on the lighting. They wanted a modern lighting system. I don't see why you have to have all that light in a church. Nobody reads the book anyway. I don't like recessed ceiling lights that are supposed to be so great. We went to England, visited all these cathedrals. I didn't see a single one that had one of these cans stuck in the ceiling. They're dark and beautiful with just daylight. In some of them they had a little table with a mirror top and you would see the ceiling reflected. Instead

of looking up, you could look down and see all the intricate carvings and castings where the ribs of the gothic vaulting met. But
with this, all you see is a big light reflection. We've cut down
about half the holes that they first wanted to do. Now we are
working on adjusting the lighting to see how it works. With any
electrical thing, I'm always worried about what fire hazards might
be created. I think modern age people require a greater light in-
tensity. We're too progressive I guess.

*Gorin: The interior of St. Patrick's is one of the great architectural
essays of New Orleans. The elements — the altar and organ loft,
the intricate system of ceiling ribs, the stained glass windows on each
side of the nave, and the three large paintings in an apse that's
covered by a massive stained glass dome — make quite a beautiful
and inspiring sight.*

Wilson: The church was originally designed by Charles B. Dakin
and James H. Dakin. They intended to have the roof vaulting span
from wall to wall without side aisle columns. The Gothic ceiling
was based on **Exeter Cathedral** [England]. James Gallier, Sr. said
in his autobiography that the Dakins withdrew from the project.
They were really fired, I guess, and Gallier became the architect.
He introduced columns to help support the roof, take some of the
load off the walls, which was probably a good idea. It certainly
made the building more attractive consisting of a nave and side
aisles with a balcony down the sides and across the back of the
church.
        Gallier apparently introduced the stained glass dome over
the altar. Dakins' apse was semi-circular and a plaster dome over
it. We've never found out if Gallier designed it to be a glass dome
as it is today. It's a very intricate construction of ribs and vaulting. Lots of the stained glass that's there today was put in around
1916. The earlier glass had been badly damaged when the church
was hit by the 1915 hurricane. We put in some steel members to
strengthen the walls and keep any movement out of it, and there
was some little spring in one or two of the ribs that we had to correct. The dome work was not a major part of the restoration.

Vieux Carré Survey

Gorin: As a missionary-preservation architect you brought to the New Orleans scene, 1961-1965, an idea for an important base-line study, the Vieux Carré Survey.[10] This research was so successful that it inspired others to produce the award winning New Orleans architectural inventory books, now seven volumes, and your friend Arch Winter to do the Natchez Survey.[11] What motivated you to tackle an in-depth study of the entire Vieux Carré, an area nearly 260 acres or about a hundred square blocks?

Wilson: The idea of making a survey of the Vieux Carré came as a result of one of the sessions of the National Trust meeting, I believe it was in Savannah or Charleston, probably Charleston [late 1950s]. One of the things brought out — to be effective in preservation you have to first know what you have to preserve by making an inventory. That impressed me. When I came back, I talked to Leonard Huber about it who was president of Louisiana Landmarks Society at the time. We presented the idea to Landmarks to make a pilot study of one square. The Society put up $500 to pay for the photographs and typing.

Leonard and I took one square of ground in the Quarter, square 63. This is the square that has the **Louisiana State Bank** — Royal, Conti, Bourbon, St. Louis. We went around and looked at every building, did research on the background of it to determine when it was built. Sometimes you find things that you didn't know existed when you research the background of it. We had photographs taken by Dan Leyrer, some photographs of Richard Koch's.[12] We made a preliminary survey to determine which buildings in that particular block were important, to give them an evaluation. We made up the initial volume.

In the case of the Quarter, most of the buildings were of either national importance, very few of those, or of architectural importance like the **Hermann-Grima House**, the **Beauregard House.** Now some of these are considered of national importance, significant locally. Some of them were interesting buildings, part of the scene. Very few were considered intrusions, the area would be better off without them. I still feel that way. There

are a few buildings that are an intrusion, but mostly they are just
shacks. In almost every building, you can find some elements of
merit that might make them part of the scene. I'd rather see them
than just a lot of big parking lots.

This question just came up a week ago. The Whitney Bank
wanted to demolish the old **John Mitchell Hotel**, St. Charles and
Common, diagonal from the **St. Charles Hotel** [now Place St.
Charles]. It's not one of the greatest buildings, but a significant
building, I think, built on the site of the old **Verandah Hotel** right
after that building was destroyed by fire in the 1850s. It's certainly better to have that building there than a big parking lot. There
are other buildings like that, not so important themselves but part
of the feeling of the whole area. We find that a lot, especially in
residential areas, like the Lower Garden District, the Garden
District.

We tried [to get a grant from] the Ford Foundation to do
the whole Vieux Carré. Bernard Lemann and I were in New York
for a Society of Architectural Historians meeting.[13] We went
over to the Ford Foundation. Great idea but too local in character. They preferred things that had wide significance; we should
try some local foundations. That's when we applied to the
Schlieder Foundation. At first, they said they didn't fund anything but medical research projects, but they took what we
showed them to their board, and their board thought it had merit.
They agreed to finance it.[14] We brought the Tulane School of Architecture into the project because the Schlieder Foundation
would only make grants to an educational institution. The
Louisiana Landmarks Society was not considered as an educational institution. We worked it out with Tulane, and they ad-
ministered the grant.

Recently, the Vieux Carré Commission wanted to have a
complete review of all the evaluations that we had done in the
Vieux Carré Survey years ago. The Commission has from time
to time reviewed some buildings, but they wanted us to review
everything. They asked the local chapter of the AIA to appoint a
committee to do this. I volunteered for it because I had been on
the original survey, so was Bernard Lemann. For the past two
years, we've been meeting about once a month in the Vieux Carré

Commission office. Hilary Irvin who is the historian for the Commission would make a preliminary review of each block, and we
would take up block after block. She would make recommendations, up graded or down graded. She would have slides of every
building in the block.

When we were doing the Survey, little shot-gun cottages
were not considered of any great importance, but they were part
of the scene and shouldn't be indiscriminately demolished. We
didn't think they were terribly important thirty years ago. Late
Victorian shot-gun cottages of the late 1880s and 1890s are now
looked on with more interest than they had at that time. So we
have upgraded them from part of the scene, yellow category, to
of architectural importance, the green category. A few have been
upgraded from architectural importance to major architectural
importance, even a few to national importance. Eean Mc-
Naughton is the chairman and the members of the committee are
Lem McCoy, "Mac" Heard, Bernard Lemann, Frank Masson,
and myself.

Historic District Demonstration Study

*Gorin: You have single-handedly pioneered the history of Gulf
South architecture. If you ever had a desire to write a history of
Vieux Carré architecture you certainly accomplished that goal in a
volume of the 1968 Historic District Demonstration Study.*[15]

Wilson: *The Vieux Carré New Orleans: Its Plan, Its Growth, Its
Architecture* was an outgrowth of the Vieux Carré Survey. The
Bureau of Governmental Research wanted to make a study for
the development of the Vieux Carré. They interviewed a lot of
urban designers and they finally gave a contract to Marcou
O'Leary [and Associates, planning and design consultants] from
Washington. The result was an eight volume series, *Historic Dis-
trict Demonstration Study.*

I was asked to do one volume on the development of the
plan of the Vieux Carré, the changes that had been made from
the time it started until the time of the study. For the final

volume, *Plan And Program For The Preservation Of The Vieux Carré,* I was asked to do a section, a condensed version, on the architecture of the Vieux Carré from the earliest French buildings to what was then the present. This volume was the result of the study in which they made certain recommendations.

Gorin: You and Mr. Koch complemented each other. As he developed his photographic skills you developed your writing skills.

Wilson: Mr. Koch had always wanted to write a history of Louisiana architecture. He worked quite a long time on it but was never satisfied with it. We finally gave his manuscript to the Southeastern Architectural Archive.

Wilson, A National Figure

Gorin: You and Mr. Koch have always been active in national professional circles which has resulted in a large national network of friends. From 1955-1965 you were on the AIA Committee on Preservation of Historic Buildings, and in 1960, you were the chairman of that committee. What were your duties as chairman?

Wilson: Now it is called the Committee on Historic Resources. Earl Reeves of Chicago was chairman of the committee when I was appointed to it. He had a sister who lived in New Orleans. He practically did nothing but run that committee. He wrote more letters. When he decided to retire, he had me appointed chairman. They usually met twice a year, generally in Washington, made up of people from all over the country. It has changed quite a bit since I was on the committee. There is a small group who runs things, but when they have a meeting in Washington almost anyone can come.

As chairman, I had to run the meetings of the committee. We talked about what important buildings were being threatened. At one of the meetings in Washington, there was a big fight about constructing big buildings around Lafayette Square. There was talk about tearing down the old **Corcoran**

Gallery [renamed **Renwick Gallery** after the architect] which faced right near the square. The committee just walked over from the **Octagon House** [AIA national headquarters]. It was just around the corner and looked at it. We decided it was an important building, and it should not be demolished. We raised cane about it, so they restored it instead of demolishing it. There were other buildings around the square. We thought some of them should be saved. We represented the feelings of the AIA all over the country wherever there was an important building being threatened, we'd take action.

There was a lot of activity at the national Capitol. They did demolish the east front and extended it out. The AIA objected to that but it went through. When they wanted to do the same thing with the west front, the AIA really raised cane. It was saved and restored. I was not involved but I may have written some letters supporting the AIA viewpoint.

Gorin: You represented the AIA in 1963 at the Williamsburg seminar. This seminar produced a report for the National Trust and Colonial Williamsburg that became influential in the passage of the National Historic Preservation Act of 1966. What stands out in your memory about that meeting?

Wilson: That was the meeting I met Mr. Adolph W. Schmidt who was the director of General Services Administration that administers all public buildings of the federal government. Meeting in Williamsburg — mostly sitting around writing up what we thought was important in the field of preservation. Mr. Schmidt was the chairman. This was when Bob Garvey was president of the Trust. Ronald Lee had been with National Park Service. Bill Murtagh was Keeper of the Register, but I don't think the Register had come in yet. Charles Peterson, Fred Rath, Charles van Ravenswaay — they were all good friends of mine. It was a general discussion to draw up some guidelines for preservation.

One evening they had a cocktail party. I met Schmidt. He knew I was from New Orleans and asked what did I think of the old **Post Office** building [on Camp Street opposite Lafayette Square]. I said I think it was one of the really important buildings of its time in New Orleans, and I think it would be a disaster to tear it down. I think when the building was designed, the front actually faced Lafayette Street, that little street, because over the top it says United States Post Office and Courthouse. I always thought the architect, who was James Gamble Rogers, intended that a similar building would be built opposite on Lafayette Street with a wide mall between them that would be on the axis of **Gallier Hall** across Lafayette Square. Smith said, "That's an interesting idea. I'm going to look it up."

The Federal government wanted to build a new federal building in New Orleans. They decided the best place to put it was on Lafayette Square and tear down the old **Post Office** building and build a new high rise. I had been involved with the old **Post Office** before. The first thing they wanted to do was take those copper figures off the roof because they said they made the roof leak.[16] There were all kinds of ideas – somebody said put them up on top of the Mississippi River bridge. Working through the Louisiana Landmarks Society, we got them not to remove those figures.

The question about removing the whole building, I was upset about it. When Schmidt went back to Washington, he researched the building and found that it was intended to face Lafayette Street. He asked me what else could we do? The space between the **Post Office** building and Poydras Street has a lot of nice interesting nineteenth century buildings, but I would rather see them go than the **Post Office** building. They tore down ten blocks of Poydras Street nineteenth buildings to widen the street from Baronne to the river. Nobody even said isn't that too bad. I did go down and take some photographs of it before they tore the things down.

Schmidt came down here the next week. I took him all through the old **Post Office** building, went up on the roof, showed him the surrounding buildings. I don't seem to have very much clout politically. They got Curtis and Davis to make a survey to recommend sites for the new building. They recommended what I had suggested – the ground. They bought that. They gave the design to Mathes and Bergman, the principal architects. They made the mall, but it didn't reflect my ideas of what I thought it should be. But it did save the building.

Gorin: Of all the battles of the 1950s and 1960s, the longest, most heated, most expensive, and very significant locally and nationally was the defeat of the elevated riverfront expressway through the Vieux Carré. Martha Robinson was the key player among many, but you were there, too.

Wilson: Yes. I spoke to the city council and wrote letters. The President's Advisory Council on Historic Preservation had been called in to rule on it. Bob Garvey was head of the committee [personal friend of Wilson's]. Now Bob Bush is the head of it. He used to be the Assistant Director of The Historic New Orleans Collection. The committee is made up of people the President thinks have an interest in the preservation of historic buildings. Maybe just Martha Robinson types, non professionals. I think some represented the National Park Service. Terry Morton was here; she represented the National Trust.

When the Advisory Council came down here, I took them on a walking tour of the site — walking down the riverfront to the **Mint**. My taking them on the tour had a lot of effect on their recommendations to the Secretary of Transportation in Washington who put the kibosh on the thing.[17]

In Conclusion

Gorin: If you had a free hand with the Vieux Carré, what would you do?

Wilson: I wouldn't want to make any radical changes in the French Quarter. I think what we are doing with the Vieux Carré Commission, trying to preserve what we have, look carefully at new things that come along, and what is done to old buildings in restoration. I wouldn't tear down the old **Civil Courts Building**. More than half a century of existence there, it has sort of taken its place in the area. It would have been well if they'd followed Richard Koch's suggestion to put a big iron fence around it like

Fig. 14. Wilson's drawing of Koch's Courthouse fence, 1941.

around the building across the street, the old **Bank of Louisiana** [344 Royal Street], or the fence around Jackson Square. He did get them to plant magnolia trees around the Courthouse which softened the harsh lines of the building, but unfortunately when some of them died, they were not replaced so you have a lot of nice big magnolia trees on the downtown side and very few on the uptown side of the building.

Gorin: How do you feel about the Jax's Brewery project, the renovation of the old brew house and the new additions?

Wilson: I think it was a good idea. I'd rather see that than have the building torn down. I don't think the second phase of the project was as successful as the first phase. It doesn't seem to have the same scale and detail that the older building has. It's not supposed to; it's a new building. The old brewery building had been there for over three quarters of a century. It was picturesque. They did a fairly good job of preserving it, adapting it. Adaptive reuse is a very important way to accomplish preservation objectives. Jax Brewery wasn't about to go back into the business of brewing beer again. The Quarter is changing.

It was a mistake in the beginning to have all the industries that have disappeared. There was a sugar refinery in one of those blocks, all kinds of commercial and industrial buildings along the riverfront. One of the worst things, [in 1879] the city gave a fifty year lease on the land across from Jackson Square, let the railroads build a big warehouse across from Jackson Square. It was as bad as the riverfront expressway that we fought so hard. I don't know that anyone objected. The city was going to collect money for this land that was not being used for anything so they put up a warehouse. It stood there for fifty years. Fortunately when the lease expired, they tore it down. Eventually they developed, for some strange reason, what was called Washington Artillery Park.

When they tore down the early **Washington Artillery Hall** on Girod Street, General Allison Owen, who was very active in the Washington Artillery, reconstructed the façade of that building on the area that had been cleared of the warehouse.[18] It was just like a piece of stage scenery. I think they·measured the façade, reconstructed it, and put the doors and windows in. The cornerstone had the name of W. A. Freret, architect. That slab was the most important fragment of the original building. The rest was a reconstruction. It stood there for years. I think the General regretted that little folly in later years. I don't know what happened to it.

Gorin: After fires and hurricanes, what in your view is another serious threat to the integrity of the historic architecture in the French Quarter?

Wilson: I think the traffic is a serious problem in the French Quarter. The old buildings were not designed to withstand the vibrations that big trucks and buses cause. I think if a riverfront roadway had been built at grade level, where the railroad tracks are, it would have probably been generally approved and might have relieved the traffic on Decatur Street for instance. The federal government had regulations that the roadway had to be above any possible flood level. That's why it was going to be elevated. That would have damaged the Quarter. At ground level it would have been behind the flood wall and you wouldn't have been conscious of it, but there wouldn't be place for the aquarium and the other things they're now planning. There's a lot of space out there especially in the upper part of the Quarter. The expressway promoters were so insistent on the elevated expressway that they wouldn't even consider a grade level road. One time they talked about a grade level road, but it wasn't grade level at all. It was elevated, too.

Gorin: Nathaniel "Buster" Curtis, Professor Curtis' son, told me that his father had a way of inspiring students to be the very best they could possibly be. You, too, have that inspiring quality. You've even won an award for being a role model (Young Leadership Council Role Model, 1987). Your career has been full of distinctive accomplishments and extraordinary contributions. Is there anything that you haven't done that you would like to do?

Wilson: One of the things I'm doing is editing the diary of Thomas K. Wharton. Wharton was an Englishman who came to New Orleans originally about 1845. He had come to this country in the 1830s, traveled around, taught at West Point. I know he was close to Colonel Sylvanus Thayer, who was superintendent of West Point, who lived up on the Hudson River area. Wharton kept a diary, and when he came down here, he resumed this diary. He lived down on Coliseum Place. Everyday he made an entry in his diary, started out with the weather, the temperature, the wind and the rain, then he'd talk about all the things that were happening in the city.

He was then architect for the **Custom House** under General Beauregard who was the official superintendent. He was on the job every day and made sketches of construction of the **Custom House** and made sketches around the city. He kept his diary until his death in 1862, which was an exciting period. He talked about the capture of New Orleans in the Civil War.

I found his diary in the New York Public Library where I guess his widow had deposited it. The library gave me permission to edit it and publish it. Tulane got a microfilm copy of it. I remember going up there and transcribing, not the whole thing but the things that related to buildings and architecture. The parts that related to the **Custom House** I thought was a separate story. Mr. Koch got interested in the diary too and said that it ought to be published. So in his will he left about $50,000.00 to The Historic New Orleans Collection to be used for the publication of the accounts of early travelers and visitors to New Orleans like the Warton Diary. The Collection actually didn't do anything about that. Finally, I wrote them a letter; that is what Mr. Koch wanted. Then they got busy and got their own microfilm copy of the diary and had it transcribed and typed. It will be published by The Historic New Orleans Collection. In the meantime they published the John H. B. Latrobe journal out of the Koch fund (Wilson 1986).[19]

Gorin: Is there "one" historic building that you have never worked on that you would like to restore?

Wilson: I would love to see the so-called Napoleon House, the **Girod House** [500 Chartres Street], restored but I don't think there's any possibility of me doing that. The building belongs to the Impastato family, but I don't think they've ever done anything in the way of restoration. That building was designed by Laclotte in 1814. That's one of the most important buildings showing continuation of the French influence in the architecture of New Orleans. It still has its original French tile roof, the iron work, the balconies. It's a great building.

The mantel in the grand salon I'm sure was done in commemoration of the battle of New Orleans. It has two trumpeting angles carved above the arch. The arch has thirteen stars carved in it. The house was being built at the time of the battle. It's [the mantel] an interesting piece of design. I haven't seen it in years. I don't know if it's still there. I hope it's still there. The **Girod House** is the one I'd most like to do!

Gorin: Your historic role model, Benjamin Latrobe, predicted in 1819 that "....it would be a safe wager that in 100 years not a vestige will remain of the buildings as they now stand except perhaps of a few public buildings & of houses built since the American acquisition of the country" (Wilson 1951:40). A hundred years from now, I hope not, but it is a possibility, not a vestige will remain of the buildings that Sam Wilson has worked on. But like Latrobe, there will be an enduring legacy of literature that you have contributed to American architectural history about a very American place, inscribed by a very American architect, Samuel Wilson, Jr. Thank you, Mr. Wilson. It is always a pleasure to talk with you.

Notes

1. During Spanish colonial administration, the local governing body or city council was called the Cabildo. The building takes it name from this council which was housed there. The **Cabildo** was used as the New Orleans City Hall from 1803-1853 when it moved into the new City Hall on Lafayette Square, now renamed **Gallier Hall**. After city government moved, the building was extensively altered to house the Supreme Court of Louisiana, 1853-1910. The Court moved when the new courthouse was completed on Royal Street, and in 1911 the **Cabildo** was given to the newly organized Louisiana State Museum which continues to use the building.

2. Martha Gilmore Robinson (1888-1981) was a founding member of Louisiana Landmarks Society and president 1958-1962. Under her leadership Kaiser Aluminum Company's proposed expansion on the site of the Battle of New Orleans, 1814-1815, resulted in Kaiser's donation of sixty-six acres to expand the National Historic Park at Chalmette, Louisiana. In 1963 Robinson won the Louise DuPont Crowninshield Award from the National Trust For Historic Preservation for her leadership of preservation activities throughout the country, especially in Louisiana, and abroad in England, Ireland, and Italy (Mulloy 1976:100).

3. William J. McCrossen, a local personality, has been with the fire department for almost fifty years and chief for seventeen years. The seventy-six year old chief responds personally to major and minor fires. He is the on-the-scene fire department spokesman for television news crews (DuBos 1990).

4. Marie-Joseph-Paul-Yves-Roch-Gilbert du Motier, Marquis de Lafayette (1757-1834), hero of the American Revolution, on tour of the United States in 1825 visited New Orleans. The city appropriated $15,000 to decorate the **Cabildo** as a residence for the distinguished visitor. City government moved out of the **Cabildo** and into a rented house that was used as a temporary city hall (Wilson and Huber 1973:71-72).

5. Wilson was the architectural component on the committee that wrote the restoration prospectus (Literary Works 1966, Wilson, Huber, de la Vergne, Bezou). The model was made in the Koch and Wilson office.

6. Robert S. Maestri (1889-1974), mayor of New Orleans 1936-1946.

7. Mayor Maestri backed the project — a crew of workers was sent from the Department of Public Works and plants came from the Parkway Commission (*The Times-Picayune* 1941).

8. Wilson married Ellen Elizabeth "Betty" Latrobe, great-great-granddaughter of Benjamin Latrobe on 20 October 1951 in the famous architect's Roman Catholic Cathedral (1804-1818, now named the **Basilica of the Assumption**) in Baltimore, Maryland.

9. **St. Patrick's** was the first church in New Orleans to be equipped with air conditioning.

10. The Vieux Carré Survey provides essential information about pieces of property in the French Quarter. The files of the Survey comprise 130 ring binders arranged by the 108 squares within the boundaries of the Vieux Carré. The Survey, which is owned by Tulane University, is on loan and housed at The Historic New Orleans Collection. The Survey was completed in the late 1960s and has been updated periodically since that time. A copy of the original survey is available on microfilm in the Southeastern Architectural Archive.

11. For the Natchez Metropolitan Planning Commission, Arch R. Winter of Mobile, Alabama, city planner for Natchez, Mississippi and a number of other cities, undertook a detailed inventory of historically and architecturally significant buildings in Natchez and the surrounding area of Adams County. Wilson was recruited for the Natchez Survey, 1972-1982, for his knowledge and aesthetic judgment. The survey has not been published to date.

12. Daniel Sweeney Leyrer (circa 1898-1978) established a photography business in New Orleans that spanned almost sixty years. Leyrer was the principal photographer for the Vieux Carré Survey. He shared a studio at 726 St. Peter Street with photographer Joseph Woodson "Pops" Whitesell. Richard Koch was an accomplished photographer and has left a trail of architectural images in archives around the city. His principal collection of 5,000 film negatives, some prints, 1915-1965, is in the Southeastern Architectural Archive. Leyrer did Koch's printing. Leyrer's principal collection is at The Historic New Orleans Collection.

13. Bernard Lemann (born 1905), now Professor Emeritus of the Tulane School of Architecture, received the Louisiana Landmarks Society 1976 Harnett T. Kane Preservation Award for his contributions to further the cause of historic preservation in New Orleans and environs — his teachings, publications, and community service. Dr. Lemann served on the board of the Vieux Carré Survey.

14. A total of $95,000.00 was granted by the Schlieder Foundation.

15. The Demonstration Study is out of print. However, *The Architecture of Colonial Louisiana*, a history in the form of a compilation of Wilson's essays, was published in 1987 (Farnsworth and Masson).

16. On the roof at each corner are twenty-five foot high sculptures, each shows a globe and female figures of history, industry, commerce, and the arts.

17. Plans for the New Orleans elevated riverfront expressway, which began in 1946 but was dormant until the 1950s, was a controversy of national importance. In 1965 the Vieux Carré became eligible for National Historic Landmark status and was therefore listed in the National Register of Historic Places. Because of this listing the New Orleans expressway fell under the provisions of the National Historic Preservation Act of 1966. Concurrently the passage of the Department of Transportation Act of 1966 created a national policy that its secretary make a special effort to preserve natural beauty of public parks and historic sites. The decision of the U.S. Secretary of Transportation, John A. Volpe, to cancel the Vieux Carré expressway, 1969, sent a message to highway builders across the nation that strong citizen opposition could radically alter long-established highway plans (Baumbach, Jr. and Borah 1981; Baumbach, Jr., personal communication, 1991.).

18. General Allison Owen (1869-1951) was one of the founders of the Tulane School of Architecture. He was the editor of *Architectural Art And Its Allies* for the life of the journal, 1905-1912. The firm of Diboll and Owen designed many public buildings in New Orleans.

19. John Latrobe (1803-1891), son of Benjamin Latrobe, was an attorney by profession and also an artist, architect, inventor, historian, and writer.

Catalog

HISTORIC ARCHITECTURAL PROJECTS
LITERARY WORKS
HONORS AND AWARDS

Fig. 15. Courtyard, Jean François Jacob House, 1930.

HISTORIC ARCHITECTURAL PROJECTS 1934-1991

The following projects of Wilson's are listed by Commission Numbers (CN) as they correspond to the Koch and Wilson Architects Commission Book. Only the long established historic districts of the Vieux Carré and Garden District are identified. Additional information given by Wilson during the compilation is included in parenthesis. New designs in historic styles are included. All files are in the Koch and Wilson office except a few which have been deposited in the Southeastern Architectural Archive, Tulane University Library. They are identified with SEAA after the CN. Some published sources by writers other than Wilson are listed.

CN 1 (Armstrong-Koch CN 225)
1950 **Le Petit Salon,** 620 St. Peter St., Vieux Carré. Alterations to the building for the addition of an elevator. (1925, Armstrong and Koch began renovation work — CN 225 in the Armstrong-Koch commission book; CN 1 in the Koch and Wilson book. This was one of the first French Quarter restoration projects, the beginning of the revitalization of the Quarter. Wilson began work on the building in 1950.)

CN 2
1934- Natchez Garden Club, **Gilreath's Hill Tavern** (1934, name according
1935   to the Historic American Buildings Survey), name changed to **Connelly's Tavern,** also called **House on Ellicott Hill,** Canal St., Natchez, Miss. Restoration of the building. (Building, 1790. 1937, opened to the public for the first time. See also CN 363)

CN 12 (Armstrong-Koch CN 144)
1938 **Trinity Episcopal Church,** 1329 Jackson Ave., Garden District. Alterations and repairs to the chapel. (1932, Koch and Armstrong began renovation work. See also CN 527, 555.)

CN 37
1936 Arts and Crafts Club, **Dr. Thomas' House,** 712 Royal St., Vieux Carré.
1939   Additions, alterations, and repairs to the building.
1941

CN 47
1937- Miss Matilda Gray, **John Gauche House,** 704 Esplanade Ave., Vieux
1938   Carré. Restoration and alterations to the house. (See also CN
1944   1621.)
            Published in:
            "The Gauche House." *The Golden Treasury of Early American
            Houses* by Richard Pratt. New York: Hawthorn Books Inc., 1968,
            2nd printing. 272-273.

CN 56 (Armstrong-Koch CN 112, SEAA)
1945- The Boston Club, **Dr. William Newton Mercer House** (town house)
1946   824 Canal St.   Interior design for a bar.   (Building designed by
            James Gallier, Sr., 1844; built for Dr. Mercer, a Natchez physician,
            philanthropist, and friend of Henry Clay. See also CN 866, 1337.)

CN 60
1969 Dr. Elizabeth Wisner and Miss Florence Sytz, 1347 Moss St. Repairs
            to the house. (1937, Koch began repairs. See also CN 897.)

CN 66
1938 The Historic New Orleans Collection, L. Kemper Williams, **Jean
            François Merieult House,** 527-533 Royal St., Vieux Carré. Res-
            toration, alterations, and repairs to the house. (See also CN 622,
            851, 1178, 1179, 1340.)

CN 68
1945- The Historic New Orleans Collection, L. Kemper Williams, 718
1946   Toulouse St., Vieux Carré. Alterations to the house to become the
            Williams' residence. (See also CN 200, 973.)

CN 73
1939- Steele Burden, 829-831 Dauphine St., Vieux Carré. Restoration of
1940   the exterior of the house; alterations to the interior for apartments.

CN 74
1938- Newcomb College, 1229 Broadway. Design of the gateway [in
1939   memory of Josephine Louise Newcomb by the class of 1904

and 1938] developed from Richard Koch's sketch. Gateway
executed by Bernard Heatherley, ironworker in Philadelphia.)

CN 83
1939 B. Manheim, **Destrehan-Perrilliat House**, 406 Chartres St., Vieux
Carré. Restoration and alterations to the interior for apartments.
(House, 1825.)

CN 97
1940 Miss Sarah Henderson, **Jean Baptiste Thierry House**, 721 Gov.
Nicholls St., Vieux Carré. Restoration and alterations of the house.
(House, 1814; Arsene Lacarrier Latour and Henry Sellon
Boneval Latrobe, architects.)

CN 98
1939- Miss Matilda Gray, 641 Barracks St., Vieux Carré. Restoration and
1941   alterations of the building. (See also CN 1621.)

CN 101
1941- William Kendall, **Monteigne** (ante-bellum mansion), Natchez, Miss.
1942   Addition of a wing to the house, playroom downstairs and bed-
rooms upstairs. (Mrs. Kendall married Hunter Goodrich see also
CN 961.)

CN 103
1940 Miss Matilda Gray, **Tailor Shop**, 640 Esplanade Ave., Vieux Carré.
Restoration and alterations to the building. (See also CN 1621.)

CN 108
1940- **Christ Church Cathedral,** 2919 St. Charles Ave. Alterations to the
1941   cathedral and the adjacent chapel. Design for the reredos
1945   and altar in the chapel and the sacristy. (Wood carving for the
reredos by Enrique Alférez, sculptor; fine wood work by Morris
Broverman, cabinet maker. See also CN 1181, 1220.)

CN 115
1941 Alvin O. King, Prien Lake, Lake Charles, La. New residence designed
in traditional Louisiana style. (King, as president of the State
Senate, suceeded Huey Long as governor of Louisiana, 1932.)

CN 123

1942 Archbishopric, **Ursuline Convent**, 1114 Chartres St., Vieux Carré. Restoration of the gate house. (See also CN 820, 936.)

CN 124

1942 Alfred Moran, Bayou Liberty, La. near Slidell. Addition of two wings
1952   to the house. (House, 1830-1840. Later sold to Temple Hargrove CN 439, named **Tranquility**.)

CN 145

1943 Miss Sarah Henderson, 723 Gov. Nicholls St., Vieux Carré. Restoration and alterations to convert the house to apartments.

CN 148

1943   Allen Wurtele, **Ramsey Plantation**, Mix, La. near New Roads. On the foundation of the old main building, a new house was designed and built in the style of the destroyed 19th century building.

CN 172

1944 Miss Matilda Gray, **Evergreen** (plantation house), Wallace, La.
1947-   Restoration of the house and outbuildings. (See also CN 1621.)
1948
        Published in:
        "Evergreen Plantation, Harold and Matilda Stream's Antebellum Estate in Louisiana." *Architectural Digest* May 1968:212-218,239.

CN 200

1945 The Historic New Orleans Collection, L. Kemper Williams, 718 and
1954   722 Toulouse St., Vieux Carré. Restored the courtyard elevations.
1958   (See also CN 68, 973, 1149, 1340.)

CN 204

1945- Frances Parkinson Keyes, **Beauregard House**, 1113 Chartres St.,
1947   Vieux Carré. Restoration of the house and alterations to the rear
1955-   wings of the house. 1947, lattice screens installed on the gallery.
1956   1961, garden pavilion constructed. (See also CN 484, 1164.)
1958
1961

CN 230

1946 Mrs. S. R. Collins, **Chester Hall** (country house), Chestertown, Md. Alterations; new entrance doorway and design for a side porch. (House, early 19th century.)

CN 248

1946 J. C. Rathborne, Harvey, La. Alterations to the houses on the Rath-
1953 borne properties. (1927, Armstrong and Koch began repairs to the 19th century properties.)

CN 249

1946 Edgar Stern, **St. Louis Hotel**, 600 St. Louis St., Vieux Carré. Historical research; supervision of the restoration drawings of the original **St. Louis Hotel**. (1835-1838, different sections of the hotel built at different times. See also 628.)

CN 261

1948 Clarence King, 535 Barracks St., Vieux Carré. Restoration and alterations to the cottage.

CN 292

1948 Louisiana State Museum, **Madame John's Legacy**, 632 Dumaine St., Vieux Carré. Repairs to the building; historical research for restoration. (House, 1788. See also CN 957.)

CN 294 SEAA

1953- Mrs. Norma Hiriart, **Bouligny House**, 1215-1217 Royal St., Vieux
1954 Carré. Alterations to the house. (See also CN 801.)

CN 300

1948 Howard B. Peabody, Jr., **Magnolia Vale**, Natchez Under the Hill, Natchez, Miss. New house built on the foundation of the 1830s structure. Some details based on those of the original house were incorporated. (**Magnolia Vale**, built by Andrew Brown, architect in Natchez, 1820s-1830s. Grounds included a large garden.)

CN 305

1953 Louise S. McGehee School, **Bradish Johnson House**, 2343 Prytania St., Garden District. Alterations to the main building; construction of a new classroom building on the property. (House, 1872. See also CN 510, 656.)

CN 313
1948 Samuel Wilson, Jr., one of a row of houses called **Freret's Folly**, 2714
      Coliseum St., Garden District. Remodeled the house. (House,
      1861; William Freret, builder. See also CN 662.)

CN 316
1948 Earl Hart Miller, **Holly Hedges** (city house), 214 Washington St.,
      Natchez, Miss. Restoration of the house. (House, circa 1820.)

CN 319 SEAA
1948 Chester A. Mehurin, 1427 Second St., Garden District. Alterations
1965 to the house. House restored after Hurricane Betsy (1965).

CN 332 (Armstrong-Koch CN 177)
1950s William Weeks Hall, **Shadows on the Teche** (plantation house), New
      Iberia, La. Design and construction of a garden pavilion or sum-
      mer house on the banks of the bayou. (House, 1831. 1927,
      Armstrong and Koch began restoration, alterations, and additions
      to the house and properties. See also CN 604, 953.)
      Published in:
      Great Georgian Houses of America Vol. II. Ralph Reinhold, chair-
      man publication committee. New York: The Scribner Press, 1937.
      23-28.
      "Eccentric master of a bayou mansion" by Marjorie Roehl. *The
      Times-Picayune* 14 July 1985:C-2.

CN 337
1951 W. M. Austin, 817 Dumaine St., Vieux Carré. Alterations to the rear
      wing which was made into apartments. (Next owner Mrs. Fairfax
      Sutter CN 1065 then Mrs. Jeanne Reagan CN 1639.)

CN 363
1947 Natchez Garden Club, **Connelly's Tavern**, Natchez, Miss. 1947,de-
1972 sign and construction of a new recreation building on the grounds
      of the historic building. 1972, a rear addition made to the new
      building. (See also CN 2.)

CN 365
1949 Frank Strachan, **Jacob U. Payne House**, 1134 First St., Garden Dis-
      trict. Alterations to the rear wing of the house. (House, circa 1850.
      See also CN 448, 625.)

Published in:
"Strachan House." *A Treasury of Early American Homes* by Richard Pratt. New York: McGraw-Hill Company Inc., 1949, 4th edition. 127.

CN 373
1949 Pilgrimage Garden Club of Natchez, **King's Tavern**, Natchez, Miss.
1971- 1949, measured drawings. 1971-1972, restoration of the building.
1972 (Possibly the earliest house in Natchez.)

CN 393
1945 Hemenway Johnson Furniture Co. Inc., **Numa Lacoste House**, 521
1950 Royal St., Vieux Carré. Restoration and alterations of the building for an antiques gallery. (House, 1859. Next owner Edith R. Stern CN 849.)

CN 401
1950 Hemenways, 526 Bourbon St., Vieux Carré. Alterations to the building; opened the property into 521 Royal St. (Bourbon St. and Royal St. properties are back to back.)

CN 404
1956- National Park Service, Chalmette National Historical Park, **René**
1958 **Beauregard House** (plantation house), Chalmette, La. Preliminary research for restoration of the house for a visitors center. "Architectural Survey Report" written for the National Park Service; supplemental report written in 1957. (Literary Works 1956b. Drawings for the restoration are with the National Park Service, Washington, D.C. See also CN 549, 1630.)

CN 409 SEAA
1951 Mrs. John T. Capo, **St. Francis Hotel**, 132-142 St. Charles Ave. at Common St. Repairs and painting of the exterior. (Hotel, late 1850s; built on the site of the old **Veranda Hotel**. The **St. Francis Hotel** became the John Mitchell Hotel. 1984, a portion of the structure was destroyed by fire.)

CN 419
1951 State Parks Commission of Louisiana, **Oakley** (plantation house), St.
1953 Francisville, La. Restoration of the house. For the Garden Clubs

1960   of America, the garden and three gates constructed from Richard
        Koch's design. 1953, drawings made for a caretaker's cottage.
        1960, repairs made to the main house.

CN 431 SEAA
1952 Carlton King, **Grace King House,** 1749 Coliseum St. Alterations to
      the house. (Carlton King, nephew of Grace King.)

CN 438
1952 Mrs. Woodruff George, 2423 Prytania St., Garden District. Re-
1955   modeled the kitchen; enclosed the upper gallery of the rear wing.
        (House, circa 1860; built for John Adams. Next owner Mrs. Hamil-
        ton Polk Jones CN 674.)

CN 439
1952 Temple Hargrove, **Tranquility,** Bayou Liberty, La. near Slidell.
      Remodeled a wing of the house for a kitchen. (Previous owner
      Alfred Moran CN 124.)

CN 448
1952 Frank G. Strachan, **Jacob U. Payne House,** 1134 First St., Garden
1962   District. Alterations to the house. Room in which Jefferson Davis
        died, partly converted to a bath and dressing room; a rear gallery
        enclosed with glass. 1962, widow's walk added on the roof. (See
        also CN 365, 625.)

CN 452
1952 Mrs. Douglas H. MacNeil, **Elms Court** (plantation house), Natchez,
      Miss. Replaced plaster ceiling center piece in the house. (See also
      CN 1264.)

CN 453
1952 Kenneth J. Colomb, 827 Toulouse St., Vieux Carré. Design for garage
      building in traditional Vieux Carré style. Unexecuted.

CN 455
1939- Le Petit Théâtre, **Orue-Pontalba House,** 616 St. Peter St., corner of
1940   Chartres St., Vieux Carré. Structural repairs to the building.
1962   1962-1963, demolition and reconstruction of the building. (See also
1963   CN 534.)

CN 456
1953   Kenneth J. Colomb, 826 Toulouse St., Vieux Carré. Drawings for an
       office building in traditional Vieux Carré style. Unexecuted.

CN 458
1953- Mrs. Douglas H. MacNeil, **Cherry Grove** (plantation house). Natch-
1954   ez, Miss. Alterations to the building.

CN 461, 461F
1953- Dr. Joseph V. Scholosser, 1240 Sixth St., Garden District. Restora-
1954   tion of the house. 1968, repairs to the house from fire damage.
1968

CN 466
1953   Ivan Purinton, **Drouet** (plantation house), Waggaman, La.   Moved
       and remodeled the house. (1991, Tchoupitoulas Plantation Res-
       taurant.)

CN 471
1953   Kenneth J. Colomb, 629 Burgundy St., Vieux Carré. Repairs to the
       cottage.

CN 472
1953   **Church of the Immaculate Conception**, Natchitoches, La. Drawings
       for the restoration of the building. Unexecuted.

CN 476
1954- Harold Levy, 812 Bourbon St., Vieux Carré. Alterations to the house.
1955
1958

CN 477
1954   Mr. and Mrs. Laurence E. Thomas, 831 Gov. Nicholls St., Vieux
       Carré. Restoration of the house.

CN 484
1954   Mrs. Frances Parkinson Keyes, **Beauregard House**, 1113 Chartres St.,
       Vieux Carré. Restoration of the garden from the original design
       discovered during the Historic American Buildings Survey. Gar-
       den not exact size of original as all buildings in the rear of the
       property could not be acquired. (Next owner Keyes Foundation
       CN 1164. See also CN 204.)

Published in:
"A peek inside the hidden garden" by Liz Scott. *Dixie* 24 November 1985:14-15.

CN 485
1954   Morgan Whitney, Bayou Liberty, La., near Slidell. Alterations and additions to the house. (When the carriage house of the **Lonsdale-McStea House**, 2521 Prytania St., was demolished, the cupola was moved to this property and converted to a service room for pool equipment. House, circa 1803; one of the oldest houses on Bayou Liberty. See also CN 838.)

CN 497
1955- Brennan's Restaurant, **Banque de la Louisiane**, 427 Royal St., Vieux
1956   Carré. Remodeled for a restaurant. (Building 1790s; **Banque de**
1958- **la Louisiane** was first bank in the Louisiana territory. See also CN
1959   573, 600.)

CN 510
1955   Louise S. McGehee School, **Bradish Johnson House**, 2343 Prytania
1959   St., Garden District. Alterations to the building. (See also CN 305,
1962   656.)
1964

CN 527
1956- Trinity Episcopal Church, 1329 Jackson Ave., Garden District. Al-
1960s terations and additions to the church and chapel; construction of two new school buildings. (See also CN 12, 555.)

CN 529
1956   Mrs. Howard B. Peabody, Sr., **Oakland** (plantation house), Natchez, Miss. Restoration of outbuildings. (See also CN 530.)

CN 530
1956   Andrew Peabody, **Oakland** (plantation house), Natchez, Miss. Restoration of the house. (Andrew Peabody, son of Mrs. Howard Peabody. See also CN 529.)

CN 534
1956   Le Petit Théâtre, 616 St. Peter St., Vieux Carré. Balcony addition to the auditorium. (See also CN 455.)

CN 549

1956 National Park Service, Chalmette National Historical Park, **René Beauregard House,** Chalmette, La. Restoration of the house for a visitors center. (See also CN 404, 1630.)

CN 552

1956 Ralph Alexis, 1015 Chartres St. (two-story building) and 611 St. Philip St. (cottage around the corner), Vieux Carré. Restoration and remodeling of both buildings. (Cottage, 1790s or earlier, brick between post construction.)

CN 555

1956 **Trinity Episcopal Church,** 1329 Jackson Ave., Garden District. Alterations and additions to the basement of the church; addition to the sacristy. (See also CN 12, 527.)

CN 559

1956 Dr. I. M. DeMatteo, **Spanish Custom House,** (small plantation
1958 house, French West Indian type), 1300 Moss St. 1956, restoration and repairs to the house. 1958, built an outbuilding. (House, 1808 or 1810.)

CN 565A, 565B

1957 M. Underwood, **Rosedown Plantation,** St. Francisville, La. Drawings for the restoration of the main house and entrance gates; design and construction of a guest cottage.

CN 567

1957 McGrew, 816 St. Philip St., Vieux Carré. Drawings for the conversion of two or three adjacent houses into a motel. Unexecuted.

CN 573

1957 Brennan's Restaurant, **Banque de la Louisiane,** 427 Royal St., Vieux Carré. Alterations to the building. (See also CN 497, 600.)

CN 579

1957- Louisiana State University, Anglo-American Art Museum, ground
1960 floor Memorial Tower, Baton Rouge campus. Designed, procured
1965 all authentic architectural elements for each gallery in the museum, both English and American wings, and installed period rooms. 1965, slight alterations. (1962, museum opened. Included in this project was a reconstruction of the exterior of Memorial Tower,

built in 1926; tower was stripped and the steel frame was rein-
forced.)
Published in:
"The Anglo-American Art Museum of Louisiana State University
in Baton Rouge" by H. Parrott Bacot. *Antiques* March 1984:637-
644.

CN 587
1958   Paul O. Pigman, 1224 Jackson Ave., Garden District. Restoration of
the house after fire damages. (Next owner Mr. and Mrs. Frederick
L. Haack CN 1281.)

CN 592
1958   Mr. and Mrs. George Morgan, 1410 Exposition Blvd. Design for a
new residence adapting elements from the **Thierry House** (CN 97).

CN 600
1958   Brennan's Restaurant, **Banque de la Louisiane**, 427 Royal St., Vieux
Carré. Additions to the building. (See also CN 497, 573.)

CN 604
1958 National Trust for Historic Preservation, **Shadows on the Teche** (plantation house), New Iberia, La. Restoration of the house and opening of the original upper rear gallery. Design and construction of
restrooms, outbuildings for visitors, William Weeks Hall's tomb;
garland wreath on the face of Hall's tomb designed by Boyd Cruise.
(Hall, 1895-1958, willed the **Shadows** with an endowment to the National Trust for Historic Preservation. See also CN 332, 953.)

CN 608
1958   Teamsters Union Local 270, 701 Elysian Fields at Royal St. Restoration, alterations, and additions. (Building, 1850s.)

CN 611 SEAA
1959   Mr. and Mrs. H. E. Breit, Jr., 1138 Third St., Garden District. Al-
1969   terations to the back building.

CN 616
1959 Maison Hospitalière, 822 Barracks St., Vieux Carré. Restoration and
alterations to rear of the Bourbon St. wing; designed and built infirmary addition; alteration to the hotel and chapel building on
Bourbon St.; renovation of a cottage on Bourbon St. (Home for

elderly women [founded in 1893]. (See also 616C, 996, 1045, 1046, 1087, 1113, 1195, 1258, 1313.)

CN 616C
1967 Maison Hospitalière, 822 Barracks St., Vieux Carré. A covered connecting link between buildings in the complex called Monroe Walk after the donor, J. Edgar Monroe. (See also 616, 996, 1045, 1046, 1087, 1113, 1195, 1258, 1313.)

CN 619
1960 Frank G. Strachan, 1118-1124 First St., Garden District. Design for a garden pavilion. Garden design by Ferdinand E. Innocenti, associate landscape architect.

CN 621
1959 City of Natchitoches, Natchitoches Main Street, Natchitoches, La. Restoration studies.

CN 622
1959 The Historic New Orleans Collection, L. Kemper Williams, 531 Royal St., Vieux Carré. Studies for an elevator and vault. Unexecuted. (See also CN 66.)

CN 624
1956 Dr. and Mrs. David W. Moore, 1538 Fourth St., Garden District. Drawings for alterations to the residence. Unexecuted. (Next owner George Farnsworth CN 772, 1192.)

CN 625
1959 Frank G. Strachan, **Jacob U. Payne House**, 1134 First St., Garden District. Garage addition; garden wall across the front. (See also CN 365, 448.)

CN 628
1959 Royal St. Louis Inc., Royal Orleans Hotel, 621 St. Louis St., Vieux Carré. In association with Curtis and Davis, architects. New construction with design features of historic **St. Louis Hotel** by J. N. B. de Pouilly (occupied the site 1835-1916) and other features of the period. All exterior designs including garage façade and pool deck. Exterior design adapted to an already designed structure. Section

of granite façade from **St. Louis Hotel** incorporated into the new Chartres St. façade.

1963   Addition of mansard roof story with dormers and balustrade; additions to the pool deck; alterations to garage entry (removed center pier to make one large opening). Dormer roof designed to be the same height as the old **St. Louis Hotel** [exceeded Vieux Carré height limitations, required special Vieux Carré commission approval]. (1991, Omni Royal Orleans Hotel. See also CN 249.)

CN 629
1959 Orleans Club, 5005 St. Charles Ave. Alterations and repairs to the building; design for the cornice in the dining room.

CN 630
1959 **Church of the Epiphany,** New Iberia, La. Consultant to Perry Segura, restoration architect.

CN 650 SEAA
1960 John Manard, 1330 Sixth St., Garden District. Alterations to the residence.

CN 656
1960 Louise S. McGehee School, 2343 Prytania St., Garden District. Design and construction of an elementary classroom building and gymnasium building on the historic property. (See also CN 305, 510.)

CN 660
1960 Dr. Robert F. Ryan, 1307 Decatur St., Vieux Carré. Alterations to the building.

CN 662
1961 Samuel Wilson, Jr., **Freret's Folly,** 2714-2716 Coliseum St., Garden District. Repairs to fire damage. (See also CN 313.)

CN 664
1961 Alfred Jay Moran, **Colonel Robert H. Short's Villa,** 1448 Fourth St., Garden District. Alterations to the house. (Alfred Jay Moran, son of Alfred Moran. Next owner Thomas Favrot CN 999.)

CN 666
1961 First Presbyterian Church, Gulfport, Miss. New church designed in Federal style. Design influenced by a church in Fincastle, Va. (See also CN 1326.)
Published in:
Palladio in Amerika by Baldur Köster. München: Prestel, 1990. 122-123.

CN 674
1961 Mrs. Hamilton Polk Jones, 2423 Prytania St., Garden District. Alterations to the house. (Previous owner Mrs. Woodruff George CN 438.)

CN 698 SEAA
1961- Dr. Peter S. Hansen, 1331 Louisiana Ave. Alterations to the house.
1962

CN 705 SEAA
1962- Mr. and Mrs. Robert Couhig, **Fairview** (plantation house). Thomp-
1963   son's Creek, La., near St. Francisville. Restoration of the house. (1963, Fairview Plantation Restaurant. House destroyed by fire about a year after restoration.)

CN 706
1962 Episcopal Bishop of Louisiana, corner Jackson Ave. and Prytania St., Garden District. Architectural studies for remodeling the bishop's residence. Unexecuted; building later demolished.

CN 707
1962 Mr. and Mrs. Fred Bunting, 714 St. Peter St., Vieux Carré. Drawings for alterations and additions. Only minor work executed. (1991, Coffee Pot Restaurant.)

CN 708
1962 Maurice M. Stern, 2226 Chestnut St. (carriage house), Garden District. Minor alterations to the house; addition of a swimming pool.

CN 710
1962 Episcopal Diocese of Louisiana, **Lavinia C. Dabney House**, 2265 St. Charles Ave., Garden District. Architectural studies for an addition to the house. (House, 1856, designed by James Gallier, Jr., of Gallier, Turpin and Co., architects-builders.)

112 Conversations with Samuel Wilson, Jr.

CN 712
1962   James J. Coleman, 627-1/2 St. Peter St., Vieux Carré. Design of a
wrought iron gate.

CN 718
1963 Louisiana State Parks and Recreation Commission, **Fort St. Jean**
1979   **Baptiste,** Natchitoches, La. 1963, prelminary studies for a replication of the colonial fort. 1979, construction of the replication.
(1938, Wilson found the original plans in the Archives Nationales,
Paris.)

CN 738
1963 Louis Fruchter, **Theodule Martin House,** 4422 Coliseum St. Alterations to the residence.

CN 744
1963 Royal St. Louis Inc., Royal Sonesta Hotel, 300 Bourbon Street, Vieux
Carré. In association with Curtis and Davis, architects. New construction with exterior design features of the existing 19th century
historic streetscape. The design process for all exterior designs
(unlike new Royal Orleans Hotel CN 628) began at start of the
project. Also design for interior public spaces: lower and upper
lobbies, arcade (not executed as designed), courtyards, Green-
house Restaurant, underground spaces. (See also CN 1615.)

CN 752
1957 Place Pontalba, 700 block Decatur St., between Jackson Square and
the River, Vieux Carré. Design for an urban park. Unexecuted.

CN 756
1964 Whitney National Bank of New Orleans, Morgan State Branch, 424-
428 Chartres St., Vieux Carré. In association with Kessels, Diboll,
Kessels, architects. Exterior design based on buildings formerly in
the same block; exterior incorporated existing granite first story;
existing granite columns and cornices supplemented with columns
from Poydras St. demolition [for Poydras corridor]. Interior vaulted ceiling inspired after J. N. B. de Pouilly's **Citizens Bank** or the
Improvement Bank in the **St. Louis Hotel** complex, Chartres and
St. Louis Streets.

CN 765

1964 Louisiana Landmarks Society, **James Pitot House,** (French colonial
1965   plantation house), 1440 Moss St. House moved and restored. 1965,
          rerestored after Hurricane Betsy (1965) damages; roof blew off and
          other damages. (Pencil drawing, 1830s by Alexandre Le Sueur,
          Museum of Natural History, LeHavre, Fr. used to restore original
          features. See also CN 1018.)
          Published in:
          "Past Present" by Pat Phillips, text; H. J. Patterson, photography.
          Dixie 16 December 1973:12,14,20,22.

CN 766

1964 **St. Patrick's Church,** 724 Camp St. Repairs and painting to interior
      of the church. (See also CN 798,1293.)
      Published in:
      "St. Patrick's Church endures on Camp Street" by Joyce M. Davis.
      The Times-Picayune/The States Item 25 August 1984:Real Estate-
      7.
      "Church's beauty works wonders" by Helen Smith. *The Times-
      Picayune/The States Item* 30 August 1986:Real Estate-1,7.
      "Answered Prayers" by Frank Schneider. *The Times-Picayune* 2
      December 1990:D-1.

CN 768

1964 Herbert Harvey and Lawrence P. Godchaux, **Gallier House,** 1132
     Royal St., Vieux Carré. Proposed restoration and alteration draw-
     ings to convert the building into apartments. Unexecuted. Under
     the same commission number, the building was remodeled for the
     residence of the next owners, Richard and Sandra Freeman. (Later
     Ella West Freeman Foundation, CN 908, 1007. 1972, New Orleans
     Chamber of Commerce Award.)

CN 772

1964 George Farnsworth, Jr., 1538 Fourth St., Garden District. Alterations
     and additions to the house. (Previous owner Dr. and Mrs. David
     W. Moore CN 624. See also CN 1192.)

CN 775

1965 Fred Lawson, 1127 Decatur St., Vieux Carré. Drawings for alterations
     to the house. Partly executed. (1967, old tile floor found under a
     rear building. This floor possibly belonged to a colonial hospital
     located on the site.)

CN 780

1965 James B. Lake, 616 Conti St., Vieux Carré. Drawings for alterations and additions to the house. Unexecuted. (House, 1820s.)

CN 786

1954 Christian Woman's Exchange, **Hermann-Grima House**, 820 St. Louis St., Vieux Carré. Alterations to the rear wing of the house. (1924, Armstrong and Koch began restoration work. See also CN 958, 1171, 1172, 1210, 1263, 1454, 1525. 1972, New Orleans Chamber of Commerce Award.)

Published in:

"Restoration of Quarter House Cited" by Jeanie Blake. *The Times-Picayune* 19 September 1971:sec. 3, 2.

"Historic House Being Restored" by Don Lee Keith. *The Times-Picayune* 14 November 1971:sec. 7, 2.

"Hermann-Grima House Has Only Restored Quarter Stable" by Stella Pitts. *The Times-Picayune* 27 October 1974:sec. 2, 15.

CN 787

1965 WDSU-TV, **François Seignouret House**, 520 Royal St., Vieux Carré.

1967 Renovations to the house including restoration of the stairway in the entrance.

CN 790

1965 New Orleans Tourist and Convention Center, American Legion Hall, **The Bank of Louisiana**, 334 Royal St., Vieux Carré. Restoration of the building with Curtis and Davis, architects. (1991, New Orleans Police Dept., Vieux Carré District. See also CN 954.)

CN 792

1965 Lawrence Williams, 3 Garden Lane. Alterations to the building, including the garden from Richard Koch's drawing. (1924, Armstrong and Koch began restoration work. House formerly located on Tchoupitoulas St. and Nashville Ave. For Isaac H. Stauffer, Armstrong and Koch took the building down, moved, and reconstructed it on Garden Lane; J. A. Haase, contractor. Next owner Ken Martin CN 1280.)

CN 797
1965   Mrs. S. Walter Stern, 1223 Philip St., Garden District.   Built an enclosed a porch. (1929, Armstrong and Koch began restoration work for Misses Sara and Mamie Butler, owners.)

CN 798
1965   **St. Patrick's Church,** 724 Camp St. Design and construction of a freestanding altar and lectern (to bring up to requirements of new liturgy); repairs to storm damage, Hurricane Betsy (1965). (See also CN 766, 1293.)

CN 801
1965   Mrs. Norma Hiriart, **Bouligny House,** 1215 Royal St., Vieux Carré. Repairs to storm damage, Hurricane Betsy (1965). (House, circa 1830. See also CN 294.)

CN 805
1965   John B. Hobson, 1224 Jackson Ave., Garden District. Repairs to storm damage, Hurricane Betsy (1965).

CN 812
1965   James J. Coleman, **Campbell House,** St. Charles Ave. and Julia St. Measured drawings of the stairs and other details that were salvaged before the house was demolished. (House, 1859, was once owned by the Poydras Asylum and was federal headquarters for Gen. Butler during the Civil War. L. E. Reynolds, architect.)

CN 813
1966   Louisiana State Museum, **Cabildo,** Jackson Square, Vieux Carré. In association with Maxwell and LeBreton, architects. Restoration and renovations. (See also CN 1665.)

CN 815
1966   Charles Keller III and Richard Freeman, Jr., 1134 Royal St., Vieux Carré. Remodeled building for apartments.

CN 816
1966   **St. Louis Basilica,** Jackson Square, Vieux Carré. Drawings for a new high altar (to bring up to requirements of new liturgy). Unexecuted.

CN 820
1966   Archbishopric, **Ursuline Convent**, 1114 Chartres St., Vieux Carré.
       New slate roof and restoration of the dormers. Designed the model
       for the proposed restoration of the building according to "Old Ur-
       suline Convent Restoration Prospectus 1966." (Literary Works
       1966, Wilson, Huber, de la Vergne, Bezou. Beginning of the res-
       toration of the building. See also CN 123, 936.)

CN 821
1966   Board of Trade, Board of Trade Plaza, 310-320 Magazine St. Design
       and construction of a small urban park including cast-iron elements
       from the **St. James Hotel** formerly on the site. (1969, AIA Award;
       1973, New Orleans Chamber of Commerce Award.)
       Published in:
       "An old alley revisted" by Karen Kingsley. *Dixie* 15 April 1984:30.

CN 825
1966   D. H. Holmes Garage, 821 Iberville St., Vieux Carré. In association
       with Kessels, Diboll, Kessels, architects. Restoration of the façades
       of three houses on the site; saved approximately twenty feet from
       the fronts and built a parking garage beside and behind façades.
       Installed an elevator in the restored section. (Houses, 1840s.)

CN 828
1966   Thomas Jordan, 1415 Third St., Garden District. Drawings for the
       remodeling of the carriage house. Unexecuted.

CN 833
1966   Louisiana State Museum, **Presbytere**, Jackson Square, Vieux Carré.
       Reroofed the building with new slates.

CN 834
1966- Redemptorist Parish, **St. Alphonsus Roman Catholic Church**, 2029
1967   Constance St. Repairs to storm damage, Hurricane Betsy (1965).

CN 838
1966   Morgan Whitney, Bayou Liberty, La., near Slidell. Alterations and
1968   additions to the country residence. (See also CN 485.)

CN 845
1966   Harreld Dinkins, Baldwin, La. Moved an old house from Franklin,
       La. to Baldwin and restored it. (House, 1840-1850, moved by float-

ing it on a barge down a bayou. House modeled after an illustration in *The Architecture of Country Houses* by Andrew Jackson Downing, noted 19th century architect, 293.)

CN 849
1967 Edith R. Stern, **Numa Lacoste House,** 521 Royal St., Vieux Carré. Alterations to the house. (Previous owner Hemenway Johnson Furniture Co., Inc. CN 393.)

CN 850
1965 William Jennings Long, 1010 Royal St., Vieux Carré. Addition of a stairway to the rear of the building.

CN 851
1967 The Historic New Orleans Collection, Kemper and Lelia Williams Fund Museum, 529 Royal St., Vieux Carré. Alterations to the building. (See also CN 66.)

CN 853
1967 Redemptorist Parish, Mother of Perpetual Help Chapel, **Lonsdale-McStea House,** 2521 Prytania St., Garden District. Repairs to the house and exterior painting.

CN 855
1965 State of Louisiana, **Pentagon Barracks,** across from state Capitol, Baton Rouge, La. Consultant to William J. Hughes, restoration architect. (Four buildings, circa 1820, were U.S. Army barracks designed in the form of a pentagon, fifth side opened to the Mississippi River. Barracks were located on the campus of, and used by, the old Louisiana State University.)

CN 857
1967 Joseph Bernstein and Frank Friedler, 615 Toulouse St., Vieux Carré. Built a new building in the Vieux Carré style for the Toulouse Theater. (1991, Toulouse Cabaret.)

CN 860
1967 Miss Alma Hammond, **Bosworth-Hammond House,** 1126 Washington Ave. Installation of an elevator. (House, 1860, built for Bosworth by Thomas K. Wharton, architect. Later owner Harry Bruns CN 1391, 1669.)

CN 861
1967 Robert Couhig, Restaurant Building, on the grounds of **Asphodel Plantation** near St. Francisville, La. Moved an old house from Jackson, La. to the **Asphodel** property to be used as a restaurant.

CN 862
1967 Dr. George Moss, **Texada Tavern**, Natchez, Miss. Restoration of the building. (House, 1790-1800.)

CN 865
1967 F. B. Ingram, **Magnon-Ingram House**, 620 Ursulines St., Vieux Carré. Restored, remodeled, and made additions to the house. (House, 1819; Claude Gurlie and Joseph Guillot, architects-builders, for Arnaud Magnon — owner of a shipyard at Ursulines St. and the river. After the shipyard was purchased by the city in 1819, Magnon built this house. This restoration is possibly the most luxurious in the Quarter.)
Published in:
"In New Orleans, The Nuances of Locale Preserved in the French Quarter" by Peter Carlsen. *Architectural Digest* November 1980:102-109.

CN 866 SEAA
1967 Boston Club, **Dr. William Newton Mercer House**, 824 Canal St.
1980 Kitchen alterations; remodeled second floor reception rooms; addition for ladies room. (See also CN 56, 1337.)

CN 868
1967 Corpus Christi Area Heritage Society, **Centennial House**, 411 N. Broadway, Corpus Christi, Tex. Consultant to James G. Rome, architect. (House, circa 1840.)

CN 872
1967 Mrs. Barbara Levy, **Christian Roselius House**, 515 Broadway. Alterations and repairs to the house. (Mrs. Levy married Dr. Clayton Edisen CN 1057.)

CN 883
1968 Chippewa Inc., Louis Sporl, Maurice Eagan, Mrs. Frank Strachan, L. Kemper Williams, Richard Koch, and Samuel Wilson, Jr., 2700-2706-2710 Magazine St. Restored and remodeled rear wings of a

row of four houses into apartments. (Buildings, circa 1850. See also CN 905.)

CN 885
1968 Gen. L. Kemper Williams, Patterson, La., near Morgan City. Measured drawings for an Acadian cottage to be moved to Williams' park.

CN 896 SEAA
1969 Franklin or St. Mary's Historical Society, **Grevenberg-Caffery House**, Franklin, La. Restored for an historical house museum.

CN 897
1969 Dr. Elizabeth Wisner and Miss Florence Sytz, 1347 Moss St. Repairs to the house. (See also CN 60.)

CN 898 SEAA
1969- Slaughter Ball, 927-929 St. Ann St., Vieux Carré. Restored and re-
1970   modeled the house for apartments.
1973

CN 905 SEAA
1969 Chippewa, Inc., 2700-2706-2710 Magazine St. Restoration and al-
1972   terations to the front buildings for apartments. (See also CN 883.)

CN 908
1969 Ella West Freeman Foundation, **Gallier House**, 1132 Royal St., Vieux Carré. Beginning of the restoration of the house for the foundation museum. (Previous owners Herbert Harvey and Lawrence P. Godchaux then Richard and Sandra Freeman CN 768. See also CN 1007.)
Published in:
"Restoring Architect Gallier's House in New Orleans" by Nadine Carter Russell. *Historic Preservation* October- December 1971:27-29.

CN 910
1969 State Parks Commission of Louisiana, **Kent House**, Alexandria, La. In association with Fred C. Barksdale, architect. Restoration of the house. (House, circa 1800.)

Published in:
"Kent Plantation House in Alexandria, Louisiana" by H. Parrott
Bacot. *Antiques* July 1984:134-141.

CN 912
1969 City of New Orleans, Jeanne d'Arc, Place de France, Foot of Canal
St. between International Trade Mart and Rivergate buildings.
Design of an urban park for an historic monument. (Copies of the
Jeanne d'Arc monument by Emmanuel Fremiet, 19th century
French sculptor, are also in Paris and Philadelphia.)

CN 915
1969 Thomas Jordan, **Dixie White House,** Pass Christian, Miss. Measured
the ruins of the house after Hurricane Camille (1969) for the purpose of restoration. Unexecuted. House demolished. (House
named in honor of President Woodrow Wilson's visit.)

CN 922
1969 Ella West Freeman Foundation, **Gallier House Complex,** buildings A
and B, 1118-1124 Royal St., Vieux Carré. Restoration of the duplicate buildings for museum offices, conference room, exhibit and
storage areas. (Houses, circa 1830. In 1890s, properties used as a
Seltzer water factory; in 1920s-1940s, used as an antique repair and
reproduction shop. See also CN 982, 1256.)

CN 927
1970 S. Walter Stern, Jr., 2306 Camp St., Garden District. New residence
designed in the Greek Revival style.
Published in:
Palladio in Amerika by Baldur Köster. München: Prestel, 1990.
112.

CN 931
1970 Mrs. John Pottharst, **Miltenberger House,** 900 Royal St., Vieux Carré.
Addition of an elevator to the rear of the building. (See also CN
1056.)

CN 936
1970 Archbishopric, **Ursuline Chapel,** 1114 Chartres St., Vieux Carré.
Consultant on the preservation of the circa 1787 walls which
belonged to the Almonester Chapel. (Walls later demolished. See
also CN 123, 820.)

CN 939
1970 Dr. and Mrs. Winston Weese, 2508 Camp St., Garden District. Proposed alterations to the house. Uexecuted.

CN 942
1970 Mr. and Mrs. Jack Scheinuk, 4613 St. Charles Ave. Restoration and alterations to the house.

CN 951
1971 French Market Corp., **French Market Complex,** Decatur St. from St. Ann St. to Ursulines St., Vieux Carré. In association with Nolan, Norman, Nolan, architects. Restoration of the Old Meat Market, 800 Decatur St. and the Old Vegetable Market, 1000 block of Decatur St.; replication of the Red Stores, 1000 N. Peters St. (1813, Old Meat Market; 1823, Old Vegetable Market; 1830, original Red Stores, located on Decatur St. between St. Philip and Dumaine Streets, was demolished in WPA renovations circa 1938. Replication of the Red Stores was suggested by Wilson as a means of creating more footage in the French Market project to make a viable financial package. 1976, American Society of Landscape Architects, Southwest Chapter Award. 1978, AIA Gulf States Award.) Published in:
"Red Stores in the Crescent" by Merikaye Presley. *Dixie* 5 January 1975:12-14.

CN 953
1971 National Trust for Historic Preservation, **Shadows on the Teche,**
t.d.   New Iberia, La. Restoration of the summer house in the garden. (Construction, a gift from Richard Koch. See also CN 332, 604.)

CN 954
1971 New Orleans Tourist and Convention Center, **The Bank of Louisiana,** 334 Royal St., Vieux Carré. Continuation of the restoration. (See also CN 790.)

CN 955
1971 Jax Brewery, 508-512 and 514-518 Toulouse St., Vieux Carré. Proposal to convert two historic buildings into office buildings. Unexecuted.

CN 956
1971 City of New Orleans, **Upper Pontalba Building,** St. Peters St. on Jackson Square, Vieux Carré. Reopened and restored galleries and courtyards which were closed by WPA renovations in the 1930s; rebuilt and restored shop doors on ground floor. Feasibility studies for painting, roof repairs, shops, air condition, fire protection, and drawings for renovation and restoration of all apartments. Henry W. Krotzer, Jr. project manager. (See also CN 1431.)

CN 957
1971 Louisiana State Museum, **Madame John's Legacy,** 632 Dumaine St., Vieux Carré. Consultant to F. Monroe Labouisse, Jr., restoration architect. (House, 1788. See also CN 292.)

CN 958
1971 Christian Woman's Exchange, **Hermann-Grima House,** 820 St. Louis St., Vieux Carré. Continuation of restoration project. (See also CN 786, 1171, 1172, 1210, 1263, 1454, 1525.)

CN 960
1971 **St. Martin of Tours Church,** St. Martinsville, La. Restoration and renovation of the interior of the church. (See also CN 1058.)

CN 961
1971 Mr. and Mrs. Hunter Goodrich, **Monteigne** (ante-bellum mansion), Natchez, Miss. Proposal for enclosure of the side porch of the house. Unexecuted. (Mrs. Goodrich formerly Mrs. William Kendell CN 101.)

CN 972
1971 Mrs. E. M. Naberschnig, **Magnolia Lane** (plantation house), River Road, Westwego, La. Restoration, alterations, and repairs to the house.

CN 973
1971 The Historic New Orleans Collection, Kemper and Leila Williams Foundation, 718 Toulouse St., Vieux Carré. Restoration of the Williams' residence. (See also CN 68, 200.)

CN 982
1972 Ella West Freeman Foundation, **Gallier House Complex,** buildings A and B, 1118-1124 Royal St., Vieux Carré. Continuation of the restoration of the duplicate buildings. (See also CN 922, 1256.)

CN 983
1973 Dr. and Mrs. James Burks, 6000 St. Charles Ave. Alterations and
1975 additions to the house and the enclosure of a side porch, swimming pool, pool house, and garage. (House, 1890s; Thomas Sully, architect. Circa 1930, Moise Goldstein, architect, made alterations to the house including the stairway for Mr. Creekmore, owner. Drawings for the stairway were made by Wilson according to a design by Frederick D. Parham.)
Published in:
"Dramatic and Distinctive Georgian Revival in New Orleans" by Bethany E. Bultman, text; Steve Hogben, photography. *Southern Accents* January-February 1984:40-51.

CN 989
1972 Henry Morrison Flagler Museum, Palm Beach, Fla. Restoration of the wrought iron gate. Proposed restoration of the wrought iron fence, unexecuted.

CN 996
1972 Maison Hospitalière, 1231-1237 Bourbon St., Vieux Carré. Continuation of restoration and remodeling of buildings in the complex. (See also CN 616, 616C, 1045, 1046, 1087, 1113, 1195, 1258, 1313.)

CN 997
1972 Pilgrimage Garden Club of Natchez, **Longwood,** (unfinished ante-bellum mansion), Natchez, Miss. Consultant for preservation of the building.

CN 998
1972 Mr. and Mrs. Ernest E. Edmundson (Elizabeth), 1014 St. Philip St., Vieux Carré. Alterations and repairs to the house; addition of a stairway in the courtyard. (See also CN 1236.)

CN 999
1972 Thomas Favrot, **Colonel Robert H. Short's Villa,** 1448 Fourth St., Garden District. Alterations to the dining room opening, new glass

doors opening on to the terrace. (Previous owner Alfred Jay Moran CN 664.)

CN 1001

1972 United Daughters of the Confederacy, Rankin St., Natchez, Miss. Measured building and prepared restoration drawings for a small building to be used as headquarters for United Daughters of the Confederacy.

CN 1007

1972 Ella West Freeman Foundation, **Gallier House**, 1132 Royal St., Vieux Carré. Continuation of the restoration project including air conditioning of the back wing. (Previous owners Herbert Harvey and Lawrence P. Godchaux, then Richard and Sandra Freeman CN 768. See also CN 908.)

CN 1009

1972 Association of Natchitoches Women for the Preservation of Historic Natchitoches, **Melrose Plantation**, Natchitoches, La. Restoration of plantation buildings executed in phases. (See also CN 1009A, 1197, 1198, 1199, 1317.)

CN 1009A

1972 Association of Natchitoches Women for the Preservation of Historic Natchitoches, **Melrose Plantation**, Natchitoches, La. Restoration of the **Yucca House**. (House, 1790-1800; possibly the original house on the plantation. See also CN 1009, 1197, 1198, 1199, 1317.)

CN 1010

1972 City of Natchez, Natchez, Miss. The Natchez Historic District Study, the official survey, with Arch R. Winter, planning consultant for the city of Natchez.

CN 1014

1972 Pilgrimage Garden Club of Natchez, **Stanton Hall**, Natchez, Miss. Repairs to the house.

CN 1018

1972 Louisiana Landmarks Society, **James Pitot House**, 1440 Moss St. Design of a formal garden for the front of the house. (See also CN 765.)

CN 1020 SEAA

1972 The National Society of the Colonial Dames of America in the State of Alabama, **Kirkbride House** (1991, **Conde-Charlotte House**), 104 Theatre St., Mobile, Ala. Restoration of the house. (When the Mobile Bay tunnel was built, the back end of the house fell apart.)

CN 1023

1972 Mrs. William Nolan, **Cherokee Plantation**, Natchitoches, La. Consultant to William King Stubbs, architect.

CN 1024

1972 Mr. and Mrs. Stanley Burkley, Natchez, Miss. (South of Natchez off Kingston Road.) New residence, design based on early houses in Natchez.

CN 1040

1973 Tom Farrell and Paul Nalty, French Eighth, 500 block Wilkinson St., Vieux Carré. Restoration of the Jax Brewery stable building as shops and designs for alteration to the Haspel Bldg., Wilkinson and Toulouse Streets. (See also CN 1333, 1401, 1410.)

CN 1045

1973 Maison Hospitalière, 822 Barracks St., Vieux Carré. Fire corrections, mostly in the infirmary, to comply with fire inspection. (See also CN 616, 616C, 996, 1046, 1087, 1113, 1195, 1258, 1313.)

CN 1046

1973 Maison Hospitalière, 822 Barracks St., Vieux Carré. Feasibility study for future development of the whole complex of buildings. (See also CN 616, 616C, 996, 1045, 1087, 1113, 1195, 1258, 1313.)

CN 1052

1973 United States General Services Administration, **Custom House**, 423 Canal St. Restoration and alterations to the building; consultant to Mathes and Bergman, architects.

CN 1056

1973 Mrs. John Pottharst, **Miltenberger House**, 900 Royal St., Vieux Carré. Alterations to the Collage Shop. (See also CN 931.)

CN 1057
1973 Mrs. Clayton Edisen, **Christian Roselius House**, 515 Broadway. Restoration and alterations to the house and additions of a cabana, pool, and gate. (Mrs. Edisen formerly Mrs. Barbara Levy CN 872.)

CN 1058
1973 **St. Martin of Tours Church**, St. Martinsville, La. Continuation of the restoration of the interior of the church. (See also CN 960.)

CN 1065
1973 Mrs. Fairfax Sutter, 817 Dumaine St., Vieux Carré. Restoration of the building for apartments. (Previous owner W. M. Austin CN 337, next owner Mrs. Jeanne Reagan CN 1639.)

CN 1066
1973 Robert Sonnier, 919 Dauphine St., Vieux Carré. Drawings for alterations to the cottage. Unexecuted.

CN 1068 SEAA
1973- Archie Casbarian, Broussard's Restaurant, 819 Conti St., Vieux Carré.
1974   Drawings for proposed alterations. Unexecuted. (Next owner Joseph Marcello CN 1115.)

CN 1069
1973 Godchaux-Henderson Sugar Refinery, Reserve, La. Alterations to a guest house on the refinery property; design for an oval drive in the front and a garden in the rear. (House, early 20th century.)

CN 1086
1972 Mrs. Rose Taquino, 619 Bourbon St., Vieux Carré. Consultant for restoration of the house.

CN 1087
1973- Maison Hospitalière, 822 Barracks St., Vieux Carré. Conversion of
1974   two identical buildings into rooms for the elderly. (Buildings, 1850s. See also CN 616, 616C, 996, 1045, 1046, 1113, 1195, 1258, 1313.)

CN 1098
1973- R. N. Campbell, **Coffield House**, Edenton, North Carolina. Resto-
1974   ration, alterations, and additions to the house. (House, 1810-1820.)

Published in:
"Edenton, N. C. The Coffield House." *Colonial Homes* January-February 1982:n.p.

CN 1100
1973 Energy Corp. of Louisiana, first client; Marathon Oil Co., second client, San Francisco (plantation house), Reserve, La. Restoration of the house. (1978, AIA Award.)
Published in:
"The restoration of San Francisco (St. Frusquin), Reserve, Louisiana" by Henry W. Krotzer, Jr. *Antiques* June 1977:1169-1203.

CN 1102
1974 Dr. Myron W. Sheen, 2216 Camp St., Garden District. Alterations to the cottage. (Building, circa 1850.)

CN 1103
1974 Texas Eastern Transmission Corp., New Hope Plantation, Donaldsonville, La. Prepared measured drawings, restoration sketches, and a project report (Literary Works 1974f). Unexecuted.

CN 1113
1974 Maison Hospitalière, 822 Barracks St., Vieux Carré. Continuation of renovations. (See also CN 616, 616C, 996, 1045, 1046, 1087, 1195, 1258, 1313.)

CN 1115
1974 Joseph Marcello, Broussard's Restaurant, 819 Conti St., Vieux Carré. Restoration, alterations, and additions to the building. (Previous client Archie Casbarian CN 1068.)

CN 1121
1974 Robert Sonnier, 1009-1011 Esplanade Ave. Restoration of the house and development of a garden and patio. (See also CN 1520.)

CN 1124
1974 Koch and Wilson Architects, 2201 Magazine St., Garden District. Restoration and alterations for architectural offices and commercial spaces. (Entrance to Koch and Wilson Architects, 1100 Jackson Ave.)

CN 1138
1974 Zeb Mayhew, **Oak Alley Plantation**, Vacherie, La. Sketches for
      remodeling and restoring **Katty House**, a plantation outbuilding.
      Unexecuted. (See also CN 1625, 1641.)

CN 1140, 1140A
1974 Dr. Russell Albright, **Lalaurie House** also known as the Haunted
t.d.   House, 1140 Royal St., and 640 Gov. Nicholls St. (back wing of Royal
      St. house), Vieux Carré. Alterations to the houses.

CN 1142
1974 Friends of the Cabildo, **Creole House** in the **Cabildo Complex**, Pirates
      Alley, Vieux Carré. Restoration of the house.

CN 1144
1974- James J. Coleman, Jr., **John Augustus Blaffer House**, 1328 Felicity
1978   St. Restoration of the house. (House, 1869; Charles Lewis Hillger,
      architect.)

CN 1145
1971 Redemptorist Parish, **St. Mary's Assumption Roman Catholic
      Church**, 2052 Constance St. In association with Nolan, Holcombe,
      Apatini, Seghers, architects. Restoration of the church. (See also
      CN 1334.)

CN 1146
1974 City of New Orleans, **Edward W. Sewell Tomb**, Lafayette Cemetery
      No. 1, Washington Ave. and Prytania St., Garden District. Restora-
      tion of the tomb. (Sewell, builder of the **St. Louis Hotel**, 1835-1838;
      hotel demolished, 1916. Other tombs see also CN 1413, 1506,
      1618.)

CN 1147
1974 Immaculate Conception Church, **Old Seminary Building**,
      Natchitoches, La. Sketches and measured drawings for proposed
      restoration of the seminary. Unexecuted.

CN 1149
1974 The Historic New Orleans Collection, Kemper and Leila Williams
      Foundation, 722 Toulouse St., Vieux Carré. Restoration of the
      house. (House, circa 1790; built for Louis Adam; building later sold
      to Claude Gurlie and Joseph Guillot, architects-builders. House

restored according to 1852 drawings found in the Notarial Archives, New Orleans. See also CN 200, 1340.)

CN 1152

1975 Mr. and Mrs. Bert S. Turner, **Live Oak** (plantation house), Weyanoke, La., near Angola. Restoration of the house.
Published in:
"Live Oak A Fondly Restored Louisiana Plantation House" by Joan Goldberger, text; Hickey-Robertson, photography. *Southern Accents* July-August 1984:46-55.

CN 1153

1975 City of New Orleans, Milton H. Latter Memorial Library, **Marks Isaacs Mansion,** 5120 St. Charles Ave. Studies for restoration of the residence and alterations and adaptations for the use of the library. Unexecuted. (Mansion, 1907. See also CN 1390.)

CN 1157

1975 Byron Humphrey, Pass Christian, Miss. Restoration of the exterior of the house from storm damage, Hurricane Camille (1969). Among the damage, portico blown off. (House, mid 19th century.)

CN 1159

1975 Mr. Christian Allenburger III, Jackson, Miss. New residence designed in the Georgian style.
Published in:
Palladio in Amerika by Baldur Köster. München: Prestel, 1990. 111.

CN 1160

1975 Chester Henderson, **Elmsley** (plantation house), Woodville, Miss. Proposed restoration, alterations, and measured drawings of the house. Unexecuted. (House, 1810-1820.)

CN 1161

1975 Virgil Browne and family, **Vacherie** (plantation house), Baldwin, La. near Franklin. Restoration and alterations to the house.

CN 1164

1975 Keyes Foundation, **Beauregard House**, 1113 Chartres St., Vieux Carré. Addition of a stairway to the courtyard. (Previous owner Frances Parkinson Keyes CN 204, 484.)

CN 1170

1975 University of Mississippi, **Rowan Oak**, William Faulkner's home, Oxford, Miss. Restoration of the house.
House featured in:
"Faulkner's Mississippi". *National Geographic* March 1989:313-339.

CN 1171

1975 Christian Woman's Exchange, **Hermann-Grima House**, 820 St. Louis St., Vieux Carré. Restored the front to its original appearance. (See also CN 786, 958, 1172, 1210, 1263, 1454, 1525.)

CN 1172

1975 Christian Woman's Exchange, **Hermann-Grima House**, 820 St. Louis St., Vieux Carré. Interior graining, including the front door. (See also CN 786, 958, 1171, 1210, 1263, 1454, 1525.)

CN 1178

1975 The Historic New Orleans Collection, 527 Royal St., Vieux Carré. Redesign of the first floor for a library, including reading room, stack room, office, and vault. (See also CN 66, 1179, 1340.)

CN 1179

1975 The Historic New Orleans Collection, 527 Royal St., Vieux Carré. Continuation of restoration. (See also CN 66, 1178, 1340.)

CN 1181

1975 **Christ Church Cathedral**, 2919 St. Charles Ave. Design and installation of the burial vault to receive the ashes of the Rt. Rev. Iveson B. Noland, 1916-1975, and design of the stone floor slab marker. (Construction of the vault, Leonard V. Huber, Jr., builder. Circa 1941, made full size drawings for the stone floor slab marker for the burial vault of the Rt. Rev. Leonidas Polk, 1806-1864. Stone carved by Rai Graner Murry, sculptor. See also CN 108, 1220.)

CN 1192

1975 George Farnsworth, 1538 Fourth St., Garden District.. Addition of a living room across the rear of the house, a swimming pool, and remodeling of kitchen. (Previous owner Dr. and Mrs. David W. Moore CN 624 see also CN 772.)

CN 1195

1975 Maison Hospitalière, 822 Barracks St., Vieux Carré. Alterations and substractions to the cottage facing 1227-1229 Bourbon St. Rear section of the building torn off and a new façade, facing the garden, was designed. (See also CN 616, 616C, 996, 1045, 1046, 1087, 1113, 1258, 1313.)

CN 1197

1976 Association of Natchitoches Women for the Preservation of Historic Natchitoches, **Melrose** (plantation house), Natchitoches, La. Proposed alterations to the main house for a caretaker's apartment. (See also CN 1009, 1009A, 1198, 1199, 1317.)

CN 1198

1978 Association of Natchitoches Women for the Preservation of Historic Natchitoches, **Melrose Plantation**, Natchitoches, La. Restoration and alterations of the **Peacock House** for visitors restrooms. (See also CN 1009, 1009A, 1197, 1199, 1317.)

CN 1199

1978 Association of Natchitoches Women for the Preservation of Historic Natchitoches, **Melrose Plantation**, Natchitoches, La. Repairs to the **African House**. (See also CN 1009, 1009A, 1197, 1198, 1317.)

CN 1202

1976 Shreveport Committee of National Society of Colonial Dames of America in the State of Louisiana, Spring Street Museum, 525 Spring St., Shreveport, La. Restoration of a bank building for use as a museum. (Building, mid 19th century.)

CN 1209

1976 Dr. and Mrs. Steve Brown III, Natochitoches, La. Restoration of the house. (House, circa 1850.)

CN 1210

1976 Christian Woman's Exchange, **Hermann-Grima House**, 820 St. Louis St., Vieux Carré. Continuation of restoration project. (See also CN 786, 958, 1171, 1172, 1263, 1454, 1525.)

CN 1212
1976 Dr. Myron W. Sheen, 3313 Prytania St., Garden District. Restoration and alterations of the house and a garden plan. (House, circa 1870.)

CN 1220
1976 **Christ Church Cathedral**, Parish House, adjacent to the Cathedral, 2919 St. Charles Ave. Alterations to the library room. (See also CN 108, 1181.)

CN 1224
1976 Natchitoches Service League, **Prudhomme-Rouquier House**, 436 Jefferson St., Natchitoches, La. Consultation and measured drawings for restoration of the house. (House, 1820 or 1830.)

CN 1235
1976 Dr. Alan Sheen, **Goldsmith-Godchaux House**, 1122 Jackson Ave., Garden District. Consultation and drawings for alterations and additions to the house. (House, 1859; Henry Howard and Albert Diettel [Sr.], architects.)

CN 1236
1976 Mr. and Mrs. Ernest E. Edmundson (Elizabeth), 1014 St. Philip St., Vieux Carré. Continuation of alterations to the house. (See also CN 998.)

CN 1245 SEAA
1976 Lafayette Insurance Co., 2123 Magazine St. Consultant on exterior paint colors.

CN 1246
1976 The Historic New Orleans Collection, 526 Bourbon St., Vieux Carré. A study including sketches for the incorporation of the Bourbon St. property into The Historic New Orleans Collection complex. Unexecuted.

CN 1256
1977 Ella West Freeman Foundation, **Gallier House Complex,** buildings A and B, 1118-1124 Royal St., Vieux Carré. Sketches for the completion of the rear wings of the buildings. Unexecuted. (See also CN 922, 982.)

CN 1258
1977 Maison Hospitalière, 822 Barracks St., Vieux Carré. Exterior painting of the building at 822 Barracks. (See also CN 616, 616C, 996, 1045, 1046, 1087, 1113, 1195, 1313.)

CN 1263
1977 Christian Woman's Exchange, **Hermann-Grima House**, 820 St. Louis St., Vieux Carré. Restoration of the 1830s kitchen including reconstruction of the ovens. (See also CN 786, 958, 1171, 1172, 1210, 1454, 1525.)

CN 1264
1977 Mrs. Douglas H. MacNeil, **Elms Court**, Natchez, Miss. Installation of an elevator in the house. (See also CN 452.)

CN 1280
1977 Ken C. Martin, 3 Garden Lane, Metairie, La. Restoration of the balustrade around the roof. (Previous owner Lawrence Williams CN 792.)

CN 1281
1977 Mr. and Mrs. Frederick L. Haack, 1224 Jackson Ave., Garden District. Drawings for alterations to the house. (Previous owner Paul O. Pigman CN 587.)

CN 1285
1977 Client?, **Krebs House**, Pascagoula, Miss. Consultant for restoration of the house. Unexecuted. (House, early 18th century; possibly the oldest house on the Mississippi coast. Measured by the Historic American Buildings Survey.)

CN 1286
1977 Mrs. John F. Tatum, **Ammadelle** (city mansion), Oxford, Miss. Consultation for repairs to the house. (Owner had the original plans by Calvert Vaux, architect.)

CN 1287
1977 Client?, **Lamar House**, Oxford, Miss. Consultation for restoration of the house and drawings for restoration of the porch.

CN 1292

1977 Mississippi Park Commission, **Fort Maurepas**, Ocean Springs, Miss. In association with Fred Wagner, architect. Replication of the colonial fort.

CN 1293

1977 **St. Patrick's Church**, 724 Camp St. Reroofing and some masonry
t.d.   repairs to the building. Major restoration to the interior. Repairs to December 1990 fire damage. (See also CN 766, 798.)

CN 1294

1977 City of Natchez, **Angeletty** (city house), Natchez, Miss. Restoration of the house. (House, 1840-1850; distinct for its Gothic dormer.)

CN 1296

1977 Mr. and Mrs. Charles M. Laird, **Mercer House** (town house), Natchez, Miss. Restoration of the house. (House, circa 1818.)

CN 1297

1977 Preservation Society of Ellicott Hill, subsidiary of the Natchez Garden Club, **Magnolia Hall**, Natchez, Miss. Restoration of the building.

CN 1302

1978 City of New Orleans, Historic District Landmarks Commission Survey (Literary Works 1979, Koch and Wilson).

CN 1312

1978 Paul McIlhenny, Sugar Mill, Avery Island, La. Consultant on the preservation of the 19th century sugar mill.

CN 1313

1978 Maison Hospitaliére, 822 Barracks St., Vieux Carré. Alterations and
t.d.   additions to the Dauphine wing, named Havard Wing after the donor. Connected the wing to the infirmary; installation of an elevator. (See also CN 616, 616C, 996, 1045, 1046, 1087, 1113, 1195, 1258.)

CN 1315

1978 J. D. White, Rankin County, Miss., outside of Jackson. New residence, design based on the **Olivier House**, an 1820 New Orleans plantation style house which was demolished in 1950.

CN 1317

1978 Association of Natchitoches Women for the Preservation of Historic Natchitoches **Melrose** (plantation house), Natchitoches, La. Renovations to the front of the main house and remodeled one of two hexagon pavilions for a caretaker's apartment. (See also CN 1009, 1009A, 1197, 1198, 1199.)

CN 1318

1978 Texas State Parks Commission, **Fulton Mansion**, Fulton Beach, Tex., north of Corpus Christi. Consultant to Turner, Rome, Boultinghouse and Associates, architects. Restoration of the mansion. (Mansion, 1872; built for Colonel Fulton by George W. Purves, architect and owner of a millwork factory in New Orleans. The building was prefabricated in New Orleans and shipped to Texas.)

CN 1320

1978 Joseph Marcello, Broussard's Restaurant, 409 Bourbon St., Vieux Carré. Sketches and proposal for remodeling of the building for apartments and rear addition for the kitchen of the restaurant. Unexecuted.

CN 1324

1978 University of Mississippi, **Barnard Observatory**, Oxford, Miss. Proposal for restoration of the observatory and the attached residence. (Buildings, circa 1850). Unexecuted.

CN 1326

1978 First Presbyterian Church, Gulfport, Miss. Courtyard designed for new church in Federal style. (See also CN 666.)

CN 1333

1978 Tom Farrell and Paul Nalty, French Eighth, 528-530 Wilkinson St., Vieux Carré. Restoration and alterations of Jax's Brewery stable for stores, offices, and apartments. (See also CN 1040, 1401, 1410.)

CN 1334

1975 Redemptorist Parish, **St. Mary's Assumption Roman Catholic Church**, 2052 Constance St. In association with Nolan, Holcombe, Apatini, Seghers, architects. Relocation of the altar and sacristy; conversion of the sacristy into a chapel. (See also CN 1145.)

CN 1337 SEAA

1978 Boston Club, **Dr. William Newton Mercer House**, 824 Canal St. Addition of an exterior stairway from the balcony to the courtyard. (See also CN 56, 866.)

CN 1340

1978 The Historic New Orleans Collection, 527 Royal and 722 Toulouse Streets, Vieux Carré. Installation of a Halon system in the library on Royal St. and in the archives on Toulouse St. (See also CN 66, 200, 1149, 1178, 1179.)

CN 1341

1978 Joseph Marcello, **Elmwood** (plantation house adapted for a restaurant), River Road, Harahan, La., near Huey P. Long Bridge. Sketches for restoration and enlargement of the house which had been destroyed by fire, December 1978. Unexecuted. (Upper story of the building destroyed by a previous fire, 3 February 1940. See also 1488, 1575.)

CN 1344

1979 Joseph Marcello, La Louisiane Restaurant, 725 Iberville St., Vieux Carré. Interior alterations to the ground floor for a restaurant. (See also CN 1546.)

CN 1353

1979 Haydel-Walk Properties, 759 Carondelet. Drawings for restoration of the commercial building. Partly executed. (Building, circa 1840)

CN 1365

1979 Alabama Historical Commission, **Fort Toulouse**, Wetumpka, Ala. Consultant for the reconstruction of the fort. Unexecuted.

CN 1371

1979 William Norman, **Eagle Hall**, 1780-1782 Prytania St.. Restoration of the commercial building. (In 1890s the building was occupied by James Wilson and Co. Grocers, Samuel Wilson, Jr.'s grandfather's business. Hinderer's Iron Works owner before Norman.)

CN 1372

1981 Jefferson Parish, **Camp Parapet**, Arlington St., near Causeway Blvd. and the river, Jefferson Parish. Restoration of a Civil War powder magazine.

CN 1383

1979 Mr. and Mrs. Chester Mehurin, 1524-1526 Third St., Garden District. Restoration, alterations, and additions to the house. (House, 1859; William Freret, architect.)

CN 1384

1979 Mrs. Joyce Doherty, Historic Natchez Foundation, 609 Franklin St., Natchez, Miss. Restoration of the two story façade of the house, formerly a furniture store. (House, circa 1818. Historic Natchez Foundation grantor for the restoration project.)

CN 1386

1979 Ben C. Toledano, 700 Carondelet St. Designed new cornice for the building based on a drawing found in the Notarial Archives, New Orleans. Also designs for exterior doors and windows. Partly executed. (Building, 1845.)

CN 1389

1980 Barbara S. Edisen, 322 Lafayette St. Restoration of the exterior of the building; remodeling of the interior for offices. (Row building, 1840s.)

CN 1390

1980 City of New Orleans, Milton H. Latter Memorial Library, **Marks Isaacs Mansion**, 5120 St. Charles Ave. Restoration of principal rooms on the ground floor; development of a children's space in the service area on the ground floor, and reading and stacks areas on the second floor. Installation of an elevator and ramp in the rear of the building. (See also CN 1153.)
Published in:
"Getting cozy with books" by Karen Kingsley. *Dixie* 11 August 1985:12-13.

CN 1391

1980 Harry D. Bruns, **Bosworth-Hammond House**, 1126 Washington Ave., Garden District. Repairs to the interior of the house. (Previous owner Miss Alma Hammond CN 860. See also CN 1669.)

CN 1400
1980   Percival T. Beacroft Jr. and Ernesto Caldiera, 514-516 St. Philip St.,
       Vieux Carré. Restoration of the building.

CN 1401
1980   Tom Farrell and Paul Nalty, French Eighth, 500 block Wilkinson St.,
       Vieux Carré. A fountain project to beautify the mall and control
       traffic. Unexecuted. (See also CN 1040, 1333, 1410)

CN 1404
1980   The Historic New Orleans Collection, 714 Toulouse St., Vieux Carré.
       Restoration of the building to house the curatorial department of
       The Historic New Orleans Collection. Connected the building to
       an existing building facing Royal St.

CN 1410
1980   Tom Farrell and Paul Nalty, French Eighth, 501 Wilkinson, Vieux
       Carré. Proposal for alterations to the building. Unexecuted. (See
       also CN 1040, 1333, 1401.)

CN 1413
1980   Save Our Cemeteries, **Jefferson Fire Co. No. 22 Tomb**, Lafayette
       Cemetery No. 1, Washington Ave. and Prytania St., Garden Dis-
       trict. Restoration of the tomb. (Other tombs see also CN 1146,
       1506, 1618.)

CN 1415
1980   Citizens National Bank, 201 Northwest Railroad Ave., Hammond, La.
       In association with Gasaway and Gossen. New building designed
       in classical style.
       Published in:
       Palladio in Amerika by Baldur Köster. München: Prestel, 1990.
       124-125.

CN 1417
1980   James Cahn, 535 Barracks, Vieux Carré. Addition of a wing to the
       house. Wilson, architect; Frank Masson, project architect.

CN 1423
1980   Mrs. Elisabeth Edmundson, 911 Dauphine St., Vieux Carré. A new
       design for the rear of the house and a design for a front entry gate.

CN 1427
1981 Board of Trade, 324 Magazine. Proposal for the restoration of the building adjacent to the Board of Trade Plaza (CN 821) and alterations for use as offices and restaurant. Unexecuted. (See also CN 1472.)

CN 1429
1981 Mr. and Mrs. Duncan Strachan and Thomas B. Favrot, **Stanley House**, 1700 block Coliseum Square. Building cut into three sections and moved to Coliseum and Polymnia Streets. Restoration of the exterior of the house. (Owners purchased and relocated a building that belonged to the New Orleans School Board on Orange and Annunciation Streets. Duncan Strachan, son of Frank Strachan.)

CN 1431
1981- City of New Orleans, **Upper Pontalba Building**, St. Peter St. on
1990 Jackson Square, Vieux Carré. Roof work; continuation of the restoration project. (See also CN 956.)

CN 1433
1981 Preservation Society of Ellicott Hill, subsidiary of the Natchez Garden Club, **William Johnson House**, Natchez, Miss. Restoration of the exterior of the front and back of the house.

CN 1437
1981 Mr. and Mrs. Jerry K. Nicholson, **El Dorado Plantation**, Pointe Coupee Parish. An analysis, a report, and consultation to prevent a railroad yard from locating adjacent to the rear of the property.

CN 1444
1981 Texas Historical Foundation, **Texas Governor's Mansion**, Austin, Tex. Drawings for a garden gazebo. Wilson, architect; Henry W. Krotzer, Jr., project architect.

CN 1445
1981 The Historic New Orleans Collection, 517-525 Tchoupitoulas St. Restoration of three Greek Revival warehouse buildings; alterations for storage area for collections, film vault, conservation laboratory, and rental space. (Buildings, 1840s, see also CN 1559.)

CN 1447
1981 Tom Farrell and Paul Nalty, French Eighth, corner of Chartres and
      Toulouse Streets, Vieux Carré. Enclosure of a parking lot with a
      wrought iron fence in traditional Vieux Carré style.

CN 1450
1981 The Historic New Orleans Collection, **Alfred Grima House**, 1604
      Fourth St., Garden District. Repairs, painting, and drawings for
      proposed restoration and renovation. (House, 1850s; remodeled,
      1880-1890.)

CN 1454
1981 Christian Woman's Exchange, **Hermann-Grima House**, 820 St. Louis
      St., Vieux Carré. Continuation of the restoration of the property.
      (See also CN 786, 958, 1171, 1172, 1210, 1263, 1525.)

CN 1466
1981 United States Custom Service, 423 Canal St. Commission to write *A
      History of the U. S. Custom House in New Orleans* (Literary Works
      1984c).

CN 1467
1981 Gordon Ewin, **Trinity Episcopal Church**, Cheneyville, La. Consul-
      tant for restoration of the church. (Building, 1850s.)

CN 1472
1981 Billy Burkenroad, Burkenroad Building, 310-324 Magazine St.
      Proposal and drawings for restoration of the buildings adjacent to
      Board of Trade Plaza (CN 821). Unexecuted. (See also CN 1427.)

CN 1482
1982 First National Bank, Gause Blvd., Slidell, La. Design of new build-
      ing in the French Colonial style of 18th century Louisiana.

CN 1488
1982 Joseph Marcello, Elmwood Lawsuit, **Elmwood** (plantation house
      adapted for a restaurant), River Road, Harahan, La., near Huey P.
      Long Bridge. Drawings of the building, including location of the
      water heater, as the building was before it was destroyed by fire in
      1978. (Drawings supported owner's lawsuit against Ruud Water
      Heaters, manufacturer of the equipment the owner claimed caused
      the fire. See also CN 1341, 1575.)

CN 1494
1982 Gretna Historical Society, **David Crocket Fire Station**, 701 Second
St., Gretna, La. Restoration of the fire station. Wilson, architect;
Robert J. Cangelosi, Jr., project architect.

CN 1495
1982 Judges of the Court?, **Criminal Courts Building,** Tulane Ave. at South
Broad St. Completion of forms to certify the building for place-
ment on the National Register of Historic Places.

CN 1497
1982 Darrell Berger, Jax Brewery, Decatur St. at Jackson Square. An historical study of all Berger properties. (See also CN 1498, 1501.)

CN 1498
1982 Darrell Berger, Jax Brewery, Decatur St. at Jackson Square. Historical certification of office buildings at 329-333-335-337 North Front
St. for income tax purpose [investment tax credit]. (See also CN
1497, 1501.)

CN 1501
1982 Darrell Berger, Jax Properties, Decatur St. at Jackson Square. Historical report on each building, 329-333-335-337, in the North Front
St. complex. (See also CN 1497, 1498.)

CN 1506
1982 Department of Louisiana State Parks, **Confederate Cemetery**, Clin-
ton, La. Repairs and stabilization of tombs in the cemetery. (Other
tombs see also CN 1146, 1413, 1618.)

CN 1520
1983 Robert Sonnier, 1009-1011 Esplanade Ave. Alterations to the rear
t.d.   wing and development of a patio and garden. (See also CN 1121.)

CN 1525
1983 Christian Woman's Exchange, **Hermann-Grima House,** 820 St. Louis
t.d.   St., Vieux Carré. Addition of a restroom in the stable building.
(See also CN 786, 958, 1171, 1172, 1210, 1263, 1454.)

CN 1532

1983   Louisiana Historical Association, **Confederate Memorial Museum,** 929 Camp St. Drawings for the development of a fire exit. Unexecuted. (See also CN 1659.)

CN 1545

1983   The Preservation Resource Center, Louisiana World Exposition (1984). A small cottage with side gallery was moved to the fair site and restored for an exhibit. Wilson, architect; Frank Masson, project architect. (Cottage, 1830s.)

CN 1546

1984   Joseph Marcello, La Louisiane Restaurant, 725 Iberville St., Vieux Carré. Repairs to damage from pipes that froze and ruptured. Wilson, architect; Robert J. Cangelosi, Jr., project architect. (See also CN 1344.)

CN 1556

1984   Mr. and Mrs. E. F. Martin, 1524 Euterpe St. Consultant for restoration of the house.

CN 1559

1984   The Historic New Orleans Collection, 521 Tchoupitoulas St. Interior renovations for tenants. (See also CN 1445.)

CN 1574

1984   Robert Bacon, Point Clear, Ala. Alterations and additions to the residence. (House, 1870s or 1880s.)

CN 1575

1984   Elmwood Nursing Home, River Road, Harahan, La. The restoration of **Elmwood** plantation house, and the development of a nursing home complex surrounding the historic building. Unexecuted. (See also CN 1341,1488.)

CN 1588

1985- Mr. and Mrs. William K. Christovich residence, **Thomas Gilmour**
1986   **House,** 2520 Prytania St., Garden District. Restoration, alterations, and renovations. (House, 1853.)

CN 1614
1986 **First Presbyterian Church,** 5401 S. Claiborne Ave. Studies for alteration to the chancel.

CN 1615
1986 Royal Sonesta Inc., 300 Bourbon St., Vieux Carré. Enlarged Begue's restaurant into the courtyard area. (See also CN 744.)

CN 1618
1986 Save Our Cemeteries, **Odd Fellows Rest Tomb,** Lafayette Cemetery No. 1, Washington Ave. and Prytania St., Garden District. Restoration of the four-tier society tomb. (See also CN 1146, 1413, 1506.)

CN 1621
1986 Mr. and Mrs. Harold Stream, **Evergreen** (plantation house), Wallace, La. and Esplanade Ave. complex consisting of five 19th century buildings, Vieux Carré. In-depth historical study of all properties including the original building contract for **Evergreen.** (Literary Works 1986b. Mrs. Stream, niece and heir of Matilda Gray. See also CN 47, 98, 103, 172.)

CN 1625
1986 Zeb Mayhew, **Oak Alley Plantation,** Vacherie, La. Renovation and repair report. (See also CN 1138, 1641.)

CN 1630
1986 National Park Service, Chalmette National Historic Park, **René Beauregard House,** Chalmette, La. Alterations and repairs. (See also CN 404, 549.)

CN 1631
1987 Mrs. Betty Wisdom, 707 Fern St. Alterations and additions.

CN 1639
1987 Mrs. Jeanne Reagan, 817 Dumaine St., Vieux Carré. Alterations and additions. (See also previous owners W. M. Austin CN 337 and Mrs. Fairfax Sutter 1065.)

CN 1641
1987 Zeb Mayhew, **Oak Alley** (plantation house), Vacherie, La. Repairs to the house. (See also CN 1138, 1625.)

CN 1642
1987 Paul S. Minor, **Louis Sullivan House**, Ocean Springs, Miss. Resto-
t.d.   ration and additions. (House perhaps designed by Frank Lloyd
         Wright, but probably Wright only followed Sullivan's design; client
         former student.)

CN 1647
1987 Dr. Dennis Riddle, La Grange, Ga. Design for a new house in colonial
         Louisiana style. (Client former student.)

CN 1653
1987 Dauphine Orleans, 415 Dauphine St., Vieux Carré. Renovation of cot-
         tage and restoration to façade.

CN 1656
1988 Dr. Robert Guyton, 1220 Chartres St., Vieux Carré. Renovation.

CN 1659
1988 Warren G. Moses Co. Inc., **Confederate Memorial Museum**, 929
         Camp St. Consultant to Moses Co. on effect of air condition sys-
         tem installation on the building. (See also CN 1532.)

CN 1665
1988 Louisiana State Museum, **Cabildo**, Jackson Square, Vieux Carré.
t.d.   Emergency repairs after fire damages of 11 May. Replication of
         third floor and rehabilitation of the building from fire and water
         damages. (See also CN 813.)
         Published in:
         "Cabildo ravaged by flames." *The Times-Picayune* 12 May 1988:1.
         "Eleven architects vying for contract on Cabildo repairs" by Alex
         Martin. *The Times-Picayune* 20 May 1988:2.
         "N.O. expert on Cabildo to repair it" by Alex Martin. *The Times-
         Picayune* 21 May 1988:1.
         "Fire at the Cabildo" by Jan White, photography. *The Historic New
         Orleans Newsletter* Fall 1988:6-7.

CN 1669
1988 Harry D. Bruns, **Bosworth-Hammond House**, 1126 Washington Ave.,
         Garden District. Roof of wing collapsed (may have been struck by
         lighting). Consultant and restoration drawings. (Previous owner
         Miss Alma Hammond CN 860. See also 1391.)

CN 1670
1988   New Orleans Area Council Boy Scouts of America, Boy Scout Ser-
        vice Center, Bayou St. John. New design based on details of old
        building on Bayou Liberty camp site.

LITERARY WORKS
1935-1991

Wilson, Samuel, Jr.

1935 "Famous Old Homes in Louisiana." *The Southern Magazine* I(11):28-29, 48.

1936 "Latrobe's Last Design." *Southern Architectural Revue* 1(4):5-8.

1938 European travel journal, 24 April-15 June. Contains photographs and few sketches by Wilson. Wilson's private library. Unpublished.

1944 "Early Aids to Navigation at the Mouth of the Mississippi River." *U.S. Naval Institute Proceedings* 70(493):278-287.

1946 "An Architectural History of the Royal Hospital and the Ursuline Convent of New Orleans." *Louisiana Historical Quarterly* 29(3):559-659.

1948 "New Orleans Ironwork." *Magazine of Art* October: 214-217.

1950 *Louisiana Landmarks Society Gallier Exhibition*. Catalog for an exhibition of the architecture of James Gallier, Sr. presented by the Louisiana Landmarks Society and the City of New Orleans in commemoration of the centennial of [old] City Hall in City Hall. Introductory note by Marion Dean Ross. [After completition of the new City Hall, 1957, old City Hall renamed Gallier Hall.] 10-19 November.

1951 Editor, introduction, and notes. *Impressions Respecting New Orleans by Benjamin Henry Boneval Latrobe*. New York: Columbia University Press.

1952a Editor. *Henry Howard Architect*. Catalog for a photographic exhibition of the architecture of Henry Howard by photographer Clarence John Laughlin; introductory note by Bernard Lemann. Presented by the Louisiana Landmarks Society and Newcomb Art School in Newcomb art gallery. 29 March-18 April.

1952b "Diocesan House (Episcopal)." *Churchwork* October:4.

1952c "Latrobe." Lecture, Friends of the Tulane University Library, 25 April. Samuel Wilson, Jr. Papers and Drawings, Southeastern Architectural Archive. Unpublished.

1953 "Buildings Formerly on the Court House Square." *Notarial Archives of Orleans Parish 1731-1953*, revised edition, by Rudolph H. Waldo, custodian of notarial records. New Orleans. Wilson's private library.

Huber, Leonard V., Garland Taylor, and Samuel Wilson, Jr.
1953 *Louisiana Purchase.* Catalog for an exhibition prepared by the Louisiana State Museum in cooperation with the Louisiana Landmarks Society. New Orleans: The Cabildo.

Lemann, Bernard and Samuel Wilson, Jr.
1953 "New Orleans Houses." *New Orleans States*, February-November. Following essays by Wilson:

> "18th Century House Boasts Legend of Lafitte" [**Lafitte's Blacksmith Shop,** 941 Bourbon St.], 14 February:26.

> "La Direction First Big Structure in Colony," 21 February:26.

> "Cottage House of 1850s Was Startling and Advanced" [**Koch-Mays House,** 2627 Coliseum St.], 28 February:26.

> "Spanish Customhouse Has Interesting History" [1300 Moss St.], 7 March:26

> "Interesting Survivor of Spanish Colonial Days" [**Orue-Pontalba House,** 616 St. Peter St.], 14 March:26.

> "Delord Sarpy House Is Important Landmark Worth Preserving" [Howard Ave. near Camp St., demolished], 21 March:26.

> "Madame John's Legacy Rooted in Early City History" [632 Dumaine St.], 4 April:26.

> "Small House on Gov. Nicholls Vestige of Greek Revival" [**Jean Baptiste Thierry House,** 721 Gov. Nicholls St.], 11 April:26.

"Sieur George's Skyscraper Is Important Landmark" **[Lemonnier House**, Royal at St. Peter Streets], 25 April:26.

"St. Mary's Rectory Undoubtedly Oldest Structure in N.O." **[Ursuline Convent**, 1114 Chartres St.], 2 May:26.

"Landmark on Gov. Nicholls Once Home of Henry Clay Kin" [620 Gov. Nicholls St.], 9 May:26.

"Grima House on St. Louis One of Best Early Examples" **[Hermann-Grima House**, 820 St. Louis St.], 16 May:14.

"Home at 1133-35 Chartres Reflects Lush 1830s" **[Soniat House**], 23 May:26.

"Beauregard House One of Most Interesting in City" [1113 Chartres St.], 30 May:26.

"Episcopal Diocese Preserving One Of Last Gallier Designed Homes" **[Lavinia C. Dabney House**, 2265 St. Charles Ave.], 13 June:26.

"House at 723 Toulouse French-Spanish Colonial Example" **[Valery Nicholas House**], 20 June:26.

"Old Suburban Plantation Residence Now on Congress Street" [617 Congress St.], 27 June:26.

"Royal St. Brick Home Synthesis Of French and American Styles" **[Dominique Bouligny House**, 1217 Royal St.], 4 July:26.

"Barracks Street Dwelling Is Typical of City Home of Early 1800s" **[Soule House**, 925 Barracks St.], 11 July:26.

"Bosque Home on Chartres St. Built in 1795" **[Bartholome Bosque House**, 617 Chartres St.], 18 July:25.

"Mercy Hospital Landmark in Danger of Destruction" **[Thomas Saulet House**, demolished], 1 August:26.

"Girod St. House Characteristically French" [not Girod St. but **Nicholas Girod House**, 504 Chartres St.], 8 August:n.p.

"3 Miltenberger Houses in Vieux Carré Have Interesting History" [900 Royal St.], 15 August:26.

"Original Bank Building Was Last Design by Architect Latrobe" [**Louisiana State Bank**, 403 Royal St.], 29 August:25.

"Typical Old La Rionda Cottage Part of City Playground" [1218 Burgundy St.], 5 September:25.

"Cornstalk Fence Home Designed in '59" [**Colonel Robert H. Short Villa**, 1448 Fourth St.], 17 October:n.p.

"Red Brick Row Houses Appeared After Purchase" [**Julia Row**, 600-648 Julia St.], 24 October:26.

"Famous La. Plantation Mansion Crumbling to Ruins Across River" [**Seven Oaks**, Westwego, La.], 14 November:24.

1954 "The De La Ronde Plantation House (1805?)." *Journal of the Society of Architectural Historians* XIII(1):24-26.

1955 "Latrobe's Custom House, New Orleans, 1807-9." *Journal of the Society of Architectural Historians* XIV(3):30-31.

1956a "The Pontalba 1850 House." *Antiques* 60(1):58-59.

1956b "Visitors Center (René Beauregard House) Chalmette National Historical Park. Architectural Survey Report." New Orleans, 24 September. Supplemental report, April 1957. Wilson's private library and Chalmette National Historical Park Ranger Station.

1957a "Louisiana's Architectural Tradition." *Louisiana Architect and Builder* June:16-25.

1957b "The New Orleans Custom House." *A Century of Architecture in New Orleans 1857-1957*, catalog for an exhibition presented by the New Orleans Chapter of the American Institute of Architects and Louisiana Landmarks Society in the Custom House. 4-31 December.

1957c Review of *Church Architecture in New France* by Alan Gowans. *Journal of the Society of Architectural Historians* XVI(1):31-32.

1958 "The Building of St. Patrick's Church." *St. Patrick's of New Orleans, 1833-1958.* Edited by Charles L. Dufour; photography by Guy F. Bernard. Commemorative essays for the 125th anniversary of St. Patrick's Church. New Orleans: St. Patrick's Parish.

1959a "The Architecture of Historic New Orleans." *Journal of the American Institute of Architects* XXII(2):32-35.

1959b *A Guide to Architecture of New Orleans 1699-1959.* New York: Reinhold Publishing. Revised edition, *A Guide to the Early Architecture of New Orleans* (1967a).

1960 WYES-TV scripts. September-December. Samuel Wilson, Jr. Papers and Drawings, Southeastern Architectural Archive. Unpublished.

1961a *The Capuchin School in New Orleans 1725.* New Orleans: Archdiocesan School Board.

1961b Foreword. *To Glorious Immortality* by Leonard V. Huber and Guy F. Bernard. New Orleans: Alblen Books.

1961c Foreword. *The Cabildo—Two Centuries of Building.* Presented by Friends of the Cabildo.

1962 "Landmarks Members Explore New Orleans." Notes for Coliseum Square and Annunciation Square Areas Tour, Louisiana Landmarks Society, 18 November. *Préservation* 5(4):5-8.

1963a "Dufilho's Pharmacy." *New Orleans Realtor* September:8, 14-15.

1963b "Louisiana Drawings by Alexandre De Batz." *Journal of the Society of Architectural Historians* XXII(2):75-89.

1963c "Vieux Carré Survey." *New Orleans Architect* April:D-E.

Huber, Leonard V. and Samuel Wilson, Jr.
1963 *The St. Louis Cemeteries of New Orleans.* Photography and design by Abbye A. Gorin; produced by Gertrude Foley Saucier. 1990, twenty-second edition. New Orleans: St. Louis Cathedral.

Wilson, Samuel, Jr.
1964a Member of committee of authors. *A Report on Principles and Guidelines for Historic Preservation in the United States.* Preservation Leaflet Series. Washington, D.C.: The National Trust for Historic Preservation. Samuel Wilson, Jr. Papers and Drawings, Southeastern Architectural Archive.

1964b "A New Vieux Carré Hotel." *New Orleans Realtor* September:6-13.

1964c "Smaller Houses of the Garden District Tour." Notes for Louisiana Landmarks Society Tour, 15 November. *Préservation* 7(4):insert page.

1964d "The Pitot House, 1370 Moss St." Wilson's private library. Unpublished.

Huber, Leonard V. and Samuel Wilson, Jr.
1964 *Baroness Pontalba's Buildings, Their Site and The Remarkable Woman Who Built Them.* New Orleans: New Orleans Chapter of the Louisiana Landmarks Society and Friends of the Cabildo.

Wilson, Samuel, Jr.
1965a "Colonial Fortifications and Military Architecture in the Mississippi Valley." *The French in the Mississippi Valley.* Edited by John Francis McDermott. Urbana: University of Illinois Press.

1965b *Plantation Houses on the Battlefield of New Orleans.* Edited by Charles L. Dufour and Leonard V. Huber. New Orleans: Battle of New Orleans 150th Anniversary Committee. Reprinted 1989 by The Samuel Wilson, Jr. Publications Fund of the Louisiana Landmarks Society, 175th anniversary edition.

1965c Letter to the editor of *The Times-Picayune* and Editorial Department/WDSU. Concerning the elevated expressway and an open view to the river, 10 December. Martha G. Robinson Papers, Box 7, Folder 13. Unpublished.

Huber, Leonard V. and Samuel Wilson, Jr.
1965 *The Basilica on Jackson Square and Its Predecessors 1727-1965.* 1972, revised; 1987, revised. New Orleans: The Basilica of St. Louis King of France.

Wilson, Samuel, Jr.
1966a "Bayou St. John Tour." For Louisiana Landmarks Society, 16 October; printed as a handout.

1966b "Antebellum Architecture of the South." Rushton Lectures, Birmingham Southern College, Birmingham, Alabama, 19 April. Samuel Wilson, Jr. Papers and Drawings, Southeastern Architectural Archive. Unpublished.

Wilson, Samuel, Jr., Leonard V. Huber, Jules de la Vergne, and Henry C. Bezou
1966 "Old Ursuline Convent Restoration Prospectus 1966." Historical background of the Convent and recommendations for its restoration and reuse. Contains illustrations from *The Times-Democrat* 16 December 1908 and Historic American Buildings Survey drawings by Wilson. Wilson's private library. Unpublished.

Wilson, Samuel, Jr.
1967a *A Guide to the Early Architecture of New Orleans.* Revision of *A Guide to the Architecture of New Orleans 1699-1959* (1959b), sponsored by Louisiana Architects Association, New Orleans Chapter of the American Institute of Architects, and Louisiana Landmarks Society. Published for the Sixteenth Annual Gulf States Regional Convention of the AIA.

1967b "Vieux Carré tours—Society of Architectural Historians." *Vieux Carré Courier* 27 October:5-8.

1968a *The Vieux Carré New Orleans: Its Plan, Its Growth, Its Architecture. Historic District Demonstration Study.* Conducted by the Bureau of Governmental Research, New Orleans, Louisiana for the City of New Orleans. December. Reprinted with corrections 28 February 1980 (1980i).

1968b "Part II, History and Architecture of the Vieux Carré." *Plan and Program for the Preservation of the Vieux Carré. Historic District Demonstration Study.* Conducted by the Bureau of Governmental Research, New Orleans, Louisiana for the City of New Orleans. [Condensed version of 1968a.]

1968c *Bienville's New Orleans: A French Colonial Capital 1718-1768.* Edited and designed by Roulhac B. Toledano; photography by New

Orleans Blue Print, Beau Bassich. New Orleans: Friends of the Cabildo.

1968d Introduction. *316 Magazine Street March 16, 1968* [Plaza Dedication, The New Orleans Board of Trade, Ltd]. Produced by Kenneth Kolb and Co.; written by Edward J. Cocke; designed by Jack Larkins; color illustrations by Joe Barrett; photography by Leon Trice, Jr. Printed by Franklin Printing.

1969a "Ignace François Broutin." *Frenchmen and French Ways in the Mississippi Valley.* Edited by John Francis McDermott. Urbana: University of Illionis Press.

1969b "Louisiana's Architectural Heritage." *The Louisiana Architect.*
1970a Following essays in the series:

"Jackson Barracks," January VIII(1):10-11.

"Academy of the Sacred Heart, Grand Coteau, Louisiana," February VIII(2):6-7.

"Destrehan Plantation, St. Charles Parish," March VIII(3):8-9.

"The Mortuary Chapel, New Orleans, Louisiana," May VIII(5):12-14.

"Le Petit Salon," May. Unpublished.

"Evergreen Plantation, Wallace, Louisiana," July VIII(7):6-7.

"Manresa – Jefferson College, Convent, Louisiana," February IX(2):10-12.

1970b "History of the Cabildo." Louisiana State Museum Official Ceremonies Marking Restoration of the Cabildo 1795-1970. Wilson's private library.

[1970c] "Merieult House History." Prepared for The Historic New Orleans Collection. Research and working papers, 144 pages, THNOC Library. Unpublished.

Huber, Leonard V. and Samuel Wilson, Jr.
1970 *The Cabildo on Jackson Square.* New Orleans:Friends of the Cabido.

Wilson, Samuel, Jr.
1971a "Gulf Coast Architecture." *Spain and Her Rivals on the Gulf Coast.* Edited by Ernest F. Dibble and Earle W. Newton. Pensacola: The State of Florida, Department of State, Historical Pensacola Preservation Board.

1971b "New Orleans, A French Colonial City." Summaries of the Lectures, The French Spirit in Early America, The Twenty-Third Annual Williamsburg Antiques Forum. 24-29 January, 31 January-5 February. Williamsburg, Va.: Colonial Williamsburg. 16-17. Wilson's private library.

1971c Review of *The Felicianas of Louisiana* by Miriam G. Reeves and *Shadows of Old New Orleans* by James Register. *Louisiana History* XII(1):84-86.

Lemann, Bernard and Samuel Wilson, Jr.
1971 *New Orleans Architecture Volume I: The Lower Garden District.* Compiled and edited by Mary Louise Christovich, Roulhac Toledano, Betsy Swanson; photography by Betsy Swanson. Gretna, La.: Friends of the Cabildo and Pelican Publishing. [1989, seven volumes. 1976, series won American Association of State and Local History Award; 1977, Alice Davis Hitchcock Book Award.]

Wilson, Samuel, Jr.
1972a "Early History of Faubourg St. Mary" and "Julia Street's Thirteen Sisters." *New Orleans Architecture Volume II: The American Sector.* Written and edited by Mary Louise Christovich, Roulhac Toledano, Betsy Swanson, Pat Holden; photography by Betsy Swanson. Gretna, La.: Pelican Publishing.

1972b Review of *Brierfield: Plantation Home of Jefferson Davis* by Frank E. Everett, Jr. *Florida Historical Quarterly* LI(2):188-189.

1972c Review of *William Butterfield* by Paul Thompson. *The Times-Picayune* 23 April:sec. 3, 9.

1972d "Fort St. Jean Baptiste of Natchitoches, A French Colonial Fort 1714-1769." 30 October. Samuel Wilson, Jr. Papers and Drawings, Southeastern Architectural Archive. Unpublished.

1973a "Fort St. Jean Baptiste de Natchitoches." *Its Proposed Reconstruction for the Louisiana State Parks and Recreation Commission.* New Orleans: Koch and Wilson. Samuel Wilson, Jr. Papers and Drawings, Southeastern Architectural Archive.

1973b Introduction. *The Autobiography of James Gallier, Architect.* New York: DaCapo Press.

1973c "Religious Architecture in French Colonial Louisiana." *Winterhur Portfolio 8.* Edited by Ian M. G. Quimby. Charlottesville: University Press of Virginia for The Henry Francis du Pont Winterthur Museum.

1974a All plaques for Orleans Parish Landmarks Commission in *Notable New Orleans Landmarks, A Pictorial Record of the Work of the Orleans Parish Landmarks Commission 1957-1974* compiled by Leonard V. Huber. Printed by Laborde Printing, New Orleans.

1974b "Almonester: Philanthropist and Builder." *The Spanish in the Mississippi Valley 1762-1804.* Edited by John Francis McDermott. Urbana: University of Illinois Press.

1974c Architectural consultant. *Nineteenth Century Mobile Architecture, An Inventory of Existing Buildings.* City of Mobile, Mobile City Planning Commission, Mobile, Ala.

1974d Introduction. *New Orleans Architecture Volume III: The Cemeteries.* Edited by Mary Louise Christovich; written by Leonard V. Huber, Peggy McDowell, Mary Louise Christovich; photography by Betsy Swanson; drawings by Doyle Gertjejansen. Gretna, La.: Pelican Publishing.

1974e "Early History." *New Orleans Architecture Volume IV: The Creole Faubourgs.* Compiled by Roulhac Toledano, Sally Kittredge Evans, Mary Louise Christovich; photography by Betsy Swanson. Gretna, La.: Pelican Publishing.

1974f "New Hope Plantation, A Historical Sketch of the House, Its Predecessors, and Its Builders." New Orleans: Koch and Wilson. Samuel Wilson, Jr. Papers and Drawings, Southeastern Architectural Archive.

1974g Review of *Architecture of Neel Reid in Georgia* by James Grady. *Journal of the Society of Architectural Historians* XXXIII(3):260.

1974h Review of *Victorian Architecture: Its Practical Aspects* by James Steven Cart. *The Times-Picayune* 4 August:sec. 3, 12.

1975a "Architecture in Eighteenth Century West Florida." *Eighteenth Century Florida and Its Borderlands*. Edited by Samuel Proctor. Gainesville: University of Florida.

1975b Foreword. *Louisiana, A Pictorial History* by Leonard V. Huber. New York: Charles Scribner's Sons.

1976a Architectural research. *Our Lady of Guadalupe Church New Orleans, The International Shrine of St. Jude* by Leonard V. Huber. 150th anniversary edition. Produced by Custombook, South Hackensack, N.J.

1976b "Louisiana Landmarks Through the Eyes of Its Past Presidents; Samuel Wilson, Jr., First President, 1950-1956." *Préservation* 19(3):3-4.

1976c "La Nouvelle Orleans: le Vieux Carré." *Les Monuments Historiques de la France* No. 2. Paris.

1977 Editorial board. *The Virginia Journals of Benjamin Henry Latrobe 1795-1798, Volume 1, 1795-1797 and Volume 2, 1797-1798*. Editor in chief, Edward C. Carter II. New Haven: Yale University Press for the Maryland Historical Society.

[1978a] "Fort Maurepas." Prososed Reconstruction of Fort Maurepas. New Orleans: Koch and Wilson. Samuel Wilson, Jr. Papers and Drawings, Southeastern Architectural Archive.

1978b Letter to the editor. Wilson's corrections to "Federal Government Legislates Restoration Technique" by F. Monroe Labouisse, Jr. in *Preservation Press* December 1977 concerning René Beauregard House at Chalmette National Historical Park. *Preservation Press* 4(3):15.

1978c Review of *The Architecture of Georgia* by Frederick Doveton Nichols. *Journal of the Society of Architectural Historians* XXXVII(3):210.

1978d Review of *The Louisiana Capitol: Its Art and Architecture* by Vincent F. Kubly. Foreword by Solis Seiferth. *Louisiana History* XIX(4):477-479.

1978e "Yale Press Publishes First Latrobe Papers." *The Times-Picayune* 26 February:sec. 3, 4.

1979a Foreword. *The Hurst House of New Orleans* by Joseph L. Ford III. Photography by Posey Photography of New Orleans. Private publication, 500 copies. Printed by Upton Creative Printing.

1979b "Holiday Tour Set for Garden District." *Preservation Press* 6(9):1.

1979c Review of *New Orleans Architecture Volume V:The Esplanade Ridge* by Mary Louise Christovich, Sally Kittredge Evans, Roulhac Toledano. Photography by Betsy Swanson. *Louisiana History* XX(1):124-125.

1979d "Das Vieux Carré: Von franzosischem Geist gepragt." *Merian* 2/32. Hamburg, Germany.

Koch and Wilson/Urban [Urban Transportation and Planning Associates]
1979 Comments by Wilson. " A Survey of Community Development in Neighborhoods to Identify Potential National Register Historic Districts and Individual National Register Properties." Text by Henry W. Krotzer, Jr.; prepared for the Historic District Landmarks Commission, City of New Orleans.

Wilson, Samuel, Jr.
1980a "Architectural Analysis of the Hermann-Grima Historic House." *Women Who Cared.* Edited by Charles L. "Pie" Dufour. New Orleans: Christian Woman's Exchange.

1980b "Architecture of Early Sugar Plantations." *Green Fields: Two Hundred Years of Louisiana Sugar.* Lafayette: The Center for Louisiana Studies, University of Southwestern Louisiana.

1980c Consulting editor and editorial board. *The Journals of Benjamin Henry Latrobe 1799-1820, From Philadelphia to New Orleans Volume 3.* Edited by Edward C. Carter II, John C. Van Horne, and Lee W. Formwalt. New Haven: Yale University Press for the Maryland Historical Society.

1980d Editorial board. *The Engineering Drawings of Benjamin Henry Latrobe.* Edited with an introductory essay by Darwin H. Stapleton. New Haven: Yale University Press for the Maryland Historical Society.

1980e "Evolution in a Historic Area's 'Tout Ensemble.'" *Old & New Architecture, Design Relationship.* Washington, D.C.: *Preservation Press.*

1980f "Pietro Cardelli, Sculptor of the Cabildo's Eagle." *Louisiana History* XXI(4):399-405.

1980g Foreword. *Lost New Orleans* by Mary Cable. New York: American Legacy Press.

1980h Foreword. *New Orleans Interiors* by Mary Louise Christovich; photography by N. Jane Iseley. New Orleans: Friends of the Cabildo— Louisiana State Museum and The Historic New Orleans Collection.

1980i Reprint with corrections. *The Vieux Carré New Orleans: Its Plan, Its Growth, Its Architecture* (1968a). Historic District Demonstration Study. Conducted by the Bureau of Governmental Research, New Orleans, Louisiana for the City of New Orleans. Reprinted by Sister Olivia Wassmer, O.S.C. in the St. Clair Monastery Printing Shop, 720 Henry Clay Ave., New Orleans for the guides of Friends of the Cabildo Walking Tours. 28 February.

1980j Review of *Bayou St. John in Colonial Louisiana* by Edna B. Freiberg; illustrations by John Chase. *Preservation Press* 7(5):5.

1980k "Von fronzosischem Geist gepragt." *Amerika, Amerika.* Hamburg: Hoffmann und Campe.

Huber, Leonard V. and Samuel Wilson, Jr.
1980 "Quarter's Architecture a Home-Bred Mixture." Rebuttal, *The Times-Picayune/The States-Item* 14 June:5.

Wilson, Samuel, Jr.
1981a Advisory editor and foreword. *New Orleans* by John R. Kemp. Sponsored by The Preservation Resource Center of New Orleans. Woodland Hills, Calif.: Windsor Publications.

1981b "Old U.S. Custom House." *Louisiana Life* 1(2):35-40.

1981c Review of *The Architecture of the United States* by G. E. Kidder-Smith with the Museum of Modern Art, 3 volumes. *The Times-Picayune* 27 December:sec. 3, 10.

Huber, Leonard V. and Samuel Wilson, Jr.
1981 *The Presbytere on Jackson Square*. New Orleans: Friends of the Cabildo.

Watson, Thomas D. and Samuel Wilson, Jr.
1981 "A Lost Landmark Revisted: The Panton House of Pensacola." *Florida Historical Quarterly* LX(1):42-50.

Wilson, Samuel, Jr.
1982a "French Fortification at Fort Rosalie, Natchez." *La Salle and His Legacy: Frenchmen and Indians in the Lower Mississippi Valley*. Edited by Patricia K. Galloway. Jackson: University Press of Mississippi.

1982b "James Gallier, Sr." and "Benjamin H. Latrobe." *Macmillan Encyclopedia of Architects*. Adolf K. Placzek, editor in chief. New York: The Free Press, division of Macmillan Publishing. 2:153-154, 611-617.

1982c Introduction. *Jackson Square Through the Years* by Leonard V. Huber. New Orleans: Friends of the Cabildo. [Also supplied architectural research for the author.]

1982d "The Will of Hilaire Boutté." *Louisiana History* XXIII(1):68-73.

1982e "The First New Orleans Cemetery." *Save Our Cemeteries* December:2-4.

1983a "The Survey in Louisiana in the 1930s." *Historic American Buildings, Structures, Sites*. Essays edited by C. Ford Peatross. Washington, D.C.: Library of Congress.

1983b Foreword. *Over New Orleans* by David King Gleason. Aerial photography by David King Gleason. Baton Rouge: David King Gleason.

1983c "Church restored, but unchanged, in its 150 years." *Clarion Herald* 28 April:7-8.

1984a "Clifton – An Ill-Fated Natchez Mansion." *Journal of Mississippi History* XLVI(3):179-189.

1984b Editorial board. *The Correspondence and Miscellaneous Papers of Benjamin Henry Latrobe Volume 1, 1784-1804.* Edited by John C. Van Horne and Lee W. Formwalt. New Haven: Yale University Press for the Maryland Historical Society.

1984c *A History of the U.S. Customhouse in New Orleans.* Prepared for U.S. Customs Service, Region V (CN 1466). Revision of *A History of the U.S. Custom House at New Orleans* by Stanley C. Arthur, 1940 (a WPA project).

1984d Introduction. *Landmarks of New Orleans.* Compiled by Leonard V. Huber. New Orleans: Louisiana Landmarks Society and Orleans Parish Landmarks Commission.

1984e "James Pitot House." *New Orleans Preservation in Print* 11(3):14-15.

1984f "Bricks and Mortar the Merieult House." *The Historic New Orleans Collection Newsletter* II(4):8.

1984g "The Cabildo in New Orleans and Its Restoration." Lecture. June. Wilson's private library. Unpublished.

1984h "Leonard V. Huber, 1903-1984." *Save Our Cemeteries*:5-6.

1985a Editorial board. *Latrobe's View of America Series III: 1795-1820.* Editor in chief, Edward C. Carter II. New Haven: Yale University Press for the Maryland Historical Society.

1985b Review of *Louisiana Church Architecture* by R. Warren Robison. *Louisiana History* XXVI(4):429-431.

1985c Review of *Quebec City: Architects, Artisians, and Builders* by A. J. H. Richardson, Genevieve Bastien, Doris Bube, and Martha Lacombe. *Journal of the Society of Architectural Historians* XLIV(3):288-289.

1985d "President's Report, 1985." *Save Our Cemeteries.*

1985e Letter to the editor. "Reasoning behind Latter Library renovation." Wilson's response to Roger Green's article in *The Times-Picayune* 6

162   *Conversations with Samuel Wilson, Jr.*

July, Real Estate section concerning adaptive reuse of the Marks Isaacs-Williams residence. *The Times-Picayune/The States-Item* 20 July:A-14.

1986a Editor, introduction, and notes. *Southern Travels: Journal of John H. B. Latrobe, 1834.* New Orleans: The Historic New Orleans Collection. [1986, award for design concept, Southern books competition of the Southeastern Library Association; designed by Michael Ledet, Word Picture Productions, New Orleans.]

1986b "An Architectural History of Evergreen Plantation and the Esplanade Avenue Complex." Commissioned (CN 1621) by Mr. and Mrs. Harold Stream. Unpublished.

1987a *The Architecture of Colonial Louisiana.* Compiled and edited by Jean M. Farnsworth and Ann M. Masson. Lafayette, La.: The Center for Louisiana Studies, University of Southwestern Louisiana.

1987b "The Howard Memorial Library and Memorial Hall." *Louisiana History* XXVIII(3):229-244.

1987c Review of *A Sesquicentennial Salute* by Mary Grace Curry. *Louisiana History* XXVIII(4):422-24.

1987d Review of *From Fort To Port: An Architectural History Of Mobile, Alabama, 1711-1918* by Elizabeth Barrett Gould. *Louisiana History* XXIX(3):313-15.

1987e Review of *Architecture in Tennessee, 1768-1897* by James Patrick. Contemporary photographs by Michael A. Tomlan. *The Southern Quarterly* XXV(2):157-158.

1987f "The Williams Residence." *The Historic New Orleans Collection Newsletter* 5(1):6.

1987g Letter to the editor. "Sharp students." Wilson comments on the high quality of Karr Junior High School students he took on a walking tour of the Garden District and Lafayette Cemetery No. 1. *The Times-Picayune* 19 May:A-10.

1988a *First Presbyterian Church History.* New Orleans: The Samuel Wilson Jr. Publications Fund of the Louisiana Landmarks Society.

1988b "Leonard Victor Huber," "Richard Koch," "James Wilson." *A Dictionary of Louisiana Biography* General editor, Glenn R. Conrad. The Louisiana Historical Association with The Center for Louisiana Studies of the University of Southwestern Louisiana. 1:413, 469-470, 854.

1988c Review of *Common Places: Readings in American Vernacular Architecture*, editors Dell Upton and John Michael Vlach. *The Southern Quarterly* XXVI(2):89-90.

1988d Review of *Holy Things and Profane Anglican Parish Churches in Colonial Virginia* by Dell Upton. *The Southern Quarterly* XXVI(4):97-98.

1988e "Priest's House in Natchez." Written for *Journal of Mississippi History*. Unpublished.

1989a "Early History." *New Orleans Architecture Volume VII: Jefferson City.* Compiled and edited by Dorothy G. Schlesinger, Robert J. Cangelosi, Jr., Sally Kittredge Reeves; photography by Walter B. Moses, Jr. Gretna, La.: Pelican Publishing.

1989b "The Architecture of Natchez before 1830." *Natchez Before 1830.* Edited by Noel Polk. Jackson: University Press of Mississippi.

1989c "Maspero's Exchange: Its Predecessors and Sucessors." *Louisiana History* XXX(2):191-220.

1989d Review of *French and Germans in the Mississippi Valley: Landscape and Cultural Traditions*, edited by Michael Roark. *Louisiana History* XXX(3):333-335.

1989e Letter to the editor. "Council OK of awning appalling." Wilson's response to the awning allowed in front of the French Market opposite Jackson Square. *The Times-Picayune* 21 April:B-10.

1989f Letter to the editor. "Preserve Whitney Plantation." Wilson's response to Formosa Plastics Corp. plan to acquire historic Whitney. *The Times-Picayune* 8 October:B-6.

1990a "The Plantation of the Company of the Indies." *Louisiana History* XXXI(2):161-191.

1990b "In Memoriam, Angela Gregory." *Préservation* 31(5):3.

1990c Review of *Southern Comfort* by Frederick Starr. *Louisiana History* XXXI(4):441-443.

1990d Letter to the editor. "Square work commendable." Wilson's praise for the Parkway and Park Commission and the Town Gardeners for the undertaking of a major restoration of the planting in Jackson Square. *The Times-Picayune* 14 May:B-8.

1991a "The Building Contract for Evergreen Plantation, 1832." *Louisiana History* XXXI(4):399-406.

1991b Letter to the editor. "A plea to save the historic Evergreen Plantation." Wilson's response to Formosa Plastics Corp. negotiations to purchase Evergreen Plantation. *The Times-Picayune* 21 January:B-6.

n.d. Card File Index To Building Contracts In Notarial Archives, 1724-1849. Abstracts of contracts; names of contractors, architects, projects, and information to locate original documents. Copies in Koch and Wilson office (most complete), Southeastern Architectural Archive, and The Historic New Orleans Collection.

n.d. "James Pitot House, 1440 Moss Street" [building moved from 1370 Moss St. to new site, 1440 Moss St., became the home of Louisiana Landmarks Society.] Wilson's private library. Unpublished.

v.d. "722 Toulouse Street." Research and working papers, Box 2 of 2, The Historic New Orleans Collection Library.

HONORS AND AWARDS
1930-1990

Samuel Wilson, Jr.

1930a **Frank C. Churchill Prize** for summer sketches, Tulane University.

1930b **Toledano Prize** for [Wilson believes] fourth year design project, A Catholic Parish Complex, Tulane Univesity.

1938 **Edward Langley Scholarship** for travel and study abroad to research the origins of Louisiana architecture, American Institute of Architects.

1939 **Silver Beaver Award** for distinguished service to boyhood and to the Boy Scouts of America. 27 November.

1950- **President, Louisiana Landmarks Society.**
1956

1955 **Fellow, American Institute of Architects**, elected for design, education, and literature.

1956 **Member, Orleans Parish Landmarks Commission**, State of Louisiana, Governor Earl K. Long. 15 November.

1958 **Public Service Award, WTIX.** 7 April.

1960a **Member, Orleans Parish Landmarks Commission**, State of Louisiana, Governor Jimmie H. Davis, 13 October.

1960b **Chairman, American Institute of Architects Committee for Preservation of Historical Buildings.**

Mr. and Mrs. Samuel Wilson, Jr.

1965 **Redemptorists Appreciation Certificate for Spiritual and Material Assistance.** Became a Redemptorists Oblate, a member of the Third Order of the Redemptorists. 2 August.

Samuel Wilson, Jr.

1968 **Citation for Significant Achievement in Historic Preservation in the United States**, National Trust for Historic Preservation in the United States. 26 October.

Richard Koch and Samuel Wilson, Jr.
1969 **Citation for Excellence in Community Architecture;** creation of the Board of Trade Plaza for the pleasure of the people of New Orleans, and for their sensitive and imaginative design of a new urban open space in an old historic setting, American Institute of Architects. 10 October.

Samuel Wilson, Jr.
1971a **Recognition of His Interest, Scholarship, and Demonstrated Expertise in the History and Architecture of New Orleans and to Serve as Special Advisor for Historic Preservation,** General Services Administration, Region 7. July.

1971b **Honorary Member, Christian Woman's Exchange.**

1972a **Recognition for His Contribution to New Orleans' Second Largest Industry, Tourism and Conventions,** Officers and Directors of the Greater New Orleans Tourist and Convention Commission. 31 July.

1972b **Honor Award** for Urban Design Concept, Vieux Carré Historic District Study, Urban Renewal Demonstration Program, Consultant, Fifth Biennial HUD [Housing and Urban Development] Awards for design excellence. 10 October.

1972c **Outstanding Contribution to the Preservation of the Colonial Era of History in Louisiana,** Louisiana Colonials Territorial Assembly. 9 November.

Richard Koch and Samuel Wilson, Jr. Architects
1972a **Award of Excellence and Special Commendation for the Restoration of the Hermann-Grima House,** Category, Restoration, Central Area Council Chamber of Commerce in New Orleans.

1972b **Award of Excellence for Outstanding Architectural Contribution in the New Orleans Area in the Design of Gallier House,** Category, Restoration, Central Area Council, Chamber of Commerce, New Orleans Area.

Samuel Wilson,
1973 **Honorary State Senator,** named by Lt. Governor James E. Fitzmorris.

Koch and Wilson
1973 **Award of Excellence for Outstanding Architectural Contribution in the New Orleans Area in the Design of the Board of Trade Building** [not building but Board of Trade Plaza], Category, Urban Design Landscaping, Central Area Council Chamber of Commerce, New Orleans Area.

Koch and Wilson Architects
1974 **Recognition of Their Contribution to the Arts in Louisiana,** Louisiana Council for Music and Performing Arts. April.

Samuel Wilson, Jr.
1974 **Business and the Arts Award,** Louisiana Council for Music and Performing Arts.

1976a **Award of Merit for His Significant and Lasting Contribution to the Preservation of Louisiana's Architectural Heritage,** American Association for State and Local History. 19 September.

1976b **Outstanding Alumni Citation,** Tulane University.

Richard Koch and Samuel Wilson, Jr. Associated Architects
1976 **Special Award for the French Market Complex,** American Society of Landscape Architects, Southwest Chapter. 9 October.

Samuel Wilson, Jr.
1977a **Harnett T. Kane Preservation Award,** Louisiana Landmarks Society. 17 April.

1977b **Order of St. Louis Medallion and Certificate for Service to St. Patrick's Church,** Archdiocese of New Orleans.

Koch and Wilson Architects
1978 **Honor Award for the Restoration of San Francisco Plantation,** Reserve, Louisiana, Twenty-fifth Anniversary of the American Institute of Architects Gulf States Regional Convention, Biloxi, Mississippi. 15 April.

Samuel Wilson, Jr.
1979a **Preservationist of the Year Award,** Louisiana Preservation Alliance, Inc. 15 July.

1979b **Certificate of Appreciation**, Louisiana Colonials, Founders Chapter.

1979c **Preservation Award**, recognition for outstanding contribution toward historic preservation in Louisiana and appreciation for making the past known and useful to the present, Foundation for Historical Louisiana, Inc.

1979d- **President, Friends of the Cabildo**.
1981

1979e **Terry-Parkerson Award**, Garden District Association.

1980a **Gratitude for His Significant Contribution to the Jambalaya Program**, New Orleans Public Library. 26 September.

1980b **Military and Hospitalier Order of St. Lazarus of Jerusalem**.

1981a **Appreciation for the Preservation of the René Beauregard House**, Chalmette National Park Association. 22 March.

1981b **Appreciation for His Contributions to the Hermann-Grima Historic House and his dedication and understand of the vision and the hope that characterizes an expanding educational museum**, Christian Woman's Exchange. 1 April.

1981c **Certificate of Merit for Outstanding Service**, City of New Orleans. 8 May.

1981d **Recognition of His Contribution to the Preparation of Volumes I, II, and IV of the Nationally Acclaimed Series on New Orleans Architecture**, The Friends of the Cabildo. 19 October.

1982a **Honorary Deputy**, Staff of Gasper J. Schiro, Register of Conveyances, State of Louisiana, Parish of Orleans. 8 January.

1982b **Member, Orleans Parish Landmarks Commission**, State of Louisiana, Governor David C. Treen. 4 November.

1982c **Chevalier de L'Ordre des Arts et Lettres,** le Ministre de la Culture [of France]. 18 November.

1982d **Citation for Notable Service to Friends Since Organization's Inception,** Friends of the Tulane University Library Board. Winter.

1983a- **Member, Conveyance Office Advisory Commision,** Staff of Gasper
1984   J. Schiro, Register of Conveyances, State of Louisiana, Parish of Orleans. 1 May 1983 to 30 April 1984.

1983b **Arthur Ross Award** for continued excellence and integrity in the application of classical ideals, Classical America. 9 May.

Koch and Wilson
1983   **Distinguished Design, Restoration, Research, and Writing,** Committee on Historic Resources of the American Institute of Architects. 23 May.

Samuel Wilson, Jr.
1984a   **Certificate of Appreciation,** City of New Orleans. 18 May.

1984b **President, Orleans Parish Landmarks Commission.** May.

1984c **Certification of Appreciation,** 1974-1984, Preservation Resource Center of New Orleans.

1984d **President, Save Our Cemeteries.**

1985a **President Emeritus,** Recognition of Thirty-six Years of Service to the Society, Louisiana Landmarks Society, 21 April.

1985b **Certificate of Appreciation** in Recognition of His Contribution to the Organization as a Board Member and President, 1984-1985, Save Our Cemeteries.

1986a **Honor Award** to the Dean of Architectural Preservation in New Orleans for the restoration of important historic architecture; leadership in the preservation movement; creative scholarly research; and fifty years of publishing architectural history of New Orleans, of Louisiana, and of the Gulf South; The University of New Orleans, The School of Urban and Regional Studies. 19 February.

1986b **Elizebeth T. Werlein Award** for distinguished contributions to the preservation of the Vieux Carré. 7 March.

1986c **Recognition for Thirty-eight Years as Adjunct Faculty Member Teaching Louisiana Architecture,** Tulane University. 19 May.

1986d **President, Louisiana Historical Association.**

1987a **Louisiana Architects Association Medal of Honor** for having significantly advanced the profession of architecture and for leadership which has inspired other architects.

1987b **Samuel Wilson, Jr. Publications Fund of Louisiana Landmarks Society** to foster a more general interest in the architectural tradition of this region and to encourage research and in publishing results.

1987c **Young Leadership Council Role Model** for distinctive accomplishments and extraordinary contributions.

1989 **Grace King Preservation Award** for significant contributions to the preservation of Louisiana cemeteries, Save Our Cemeteries, Inc. 4 November.

1990a **The American Institute of Architects, Presidential Citation.** February.

1990b **Doctor of Humane Letters,** Tulane University 12 May.

1990c **President, The Keyes Foundation.** May.

BIBLIOGRAPHY

Baumbach, Richard O. Jr.
1991 Personal communication. 11 April.

Baumbach, Richard O. Jr. and William E. Borah
1981 *The Second Battle of New Orleans, A History of the Riverfront Expressway Controversy.* University of Alabama: The University of Alabama Press.

Carlsen, Pete
1980 "In New Orleans The Nuances of Locale Preserved in the French Quarter." *Architectural Digest* 37(9):102-109.

DuBos, Clancy
1990 "Keeper Of The Flames." *Gambit* 18 December:15-16.

Farnet, S. Stewart
1986 Speech on the occasion of Samuel Wilson, Jr.'s Golden Anniversary of Publishing, sponsored by the School of Urban and Regional Studies, University of New Orleans, McFarland Center, Southern Baptist Hospital. 19 February. Copy in possession of the author.

Farnsworth, Jean M. and Ann M. Masson, compilers and editors
1987 *The Architecture of Colonial Louisiana.* Lafayette, Louisiana: The Center for Louisiana Studies, University of Southwestern Louisiana.

Friends of the Cabildo
1972 Oral History Collection, approximately 400 interviews recorded on
t.d.   audio tapes. Speakers discuss aspects of their lives — how they lived, what they did, interesting occurances, and significant people they knew. Louisiana State Museum, Louisiana Historical Center, Old U.S. Mint, 400 Esplanade Avenue, New Orleans.

Gorin, Abbye A.
1986a Researcher-writer. Barbara Coleman, producer-director. *Samuel Wilson, Jr., Dean Of Architectural Preservation In New Orleans.* Thirty minute video documentary. Wilson tells the story of the preservation movement in New Orleans as seen through his career. Features William R. Cullison III, Charles L."Pie" Dufour, Angela Gregory, Ann M. Masson, Ray C. Samuel. Broadcast on WLAE-TV, New Orleans,

26 February. Copy in Southeastern Architectural Archive, Tulane
Library.

1986b- Audio taped recordings of Samuel Wilson, Jr. discussing aspects of
1990   his historic preservation philosophy and projects. Tapes in
        possession of the author.

1989 "Samuel Wilson, Jr., A Contribution to the Preservation of Architecture
     in New Orleans and the Gulf South". Ph.D. diss., Virginia Polytechnic
     Institute and State University. Copy in Southeastern Architectural Ar-
     chive.

Hosmer, Charles B. Jr.
1965 *Presence of the Past, A History of the Preservation Movement in theUnited
      States Before Williamsburg.* New York: G. P. Putnam's Sons.

1981 *Preservation Comes of Age, From Williamsburg to the National Trust, 1926-
      1949 Volumes I and II. Charlottesville: Published for The Preservation
      Press by the University Press of Virginia.*

Klein, Gerda Weissmann
1984 *A Passion for Sharing, The Life Of Edith Rosenwald Stern.* New York:
      Rossell Books.

Mulloy, Elizabeth D. Mulloy
1976 *The History Of The National Trust For Historic Preservation 1963-1973.*
      Washington, D.C.: The Preservation Press.

Wilson, Samuel Jr.
1944 "Early Aids to Navigation at the Mouth of the Mississippi River."*United
      States Naval Institute Proceedings* 70(493):278-287.

1951 Editor and introduction. *Impressions Respecting New Orleans by Ben-
      jamin Henry Boneval Latrobe.* New York: Columbia University Press.

1974 Introduction. *New Orleans Architecture Volume III, The Cemeteries. Gret-
      na: Pelican Publishing Company.*

1982 "Benjamin H. Latrobe" and "James Gallier, Sr." *Macmillan Encylopedia
      Of Architects,* Volume 2. New York: The Free Press.

1986 Editor and introduction. *Southern Travels, Journal Of John H. B. Latrobe, 1834.* The Historic New Orleans Collection.

Wilson, Samuel Jr. and Leonard V. Huber
1973 *The Cabildo On Jackson Square.* Gretna: Pelican Publishing Company.

n.a.
1941 "Original Garden Of City Is Laid Out In Replica." *The Times Picayune,* 17 March:6.

1970 "Ancient Building Was First N.O. Church, Ursuline Chapel to Be Restored." *New Orleans States-Item* 14 May:29.

1976 Photograph of memorial plaque honoring Clay Shaw and caption. *The Times-Picayune,* 30 September.

Suggested References

Anderson, Sherwood
1922 "New Orleans, The Double Dealer and the Modern Movement in America." *The Double Dealer III(15):119-126.*

Bercé, Françoise and Bruno Foucart
1988 *Viollet-le-Duc, Architect, Artist, Master Of Historic Preservation. Washington, D.C.: The Trust for Museum Exhibitions.*

Corn, Joseph J. and Brian Horrigan
1984 *Yesterday's Tomorrows.* Edited by Katherine Chambers. New York: Summit Books.

Cullinson, William R. III
1978 *Louisiana Landmarks Society, The First Thirty Years.* New Orleans: *Louisiana Landmarks Society.*

1983 *Architecture In Louisiana, A Documentary History.* Catalog for exhibit, Southeastern Architectural Archive, 29 May-31 December.

Genthe, Arnold
1926 *Impressions of Old New Orleans.* New York: George H. Doran.

Gorin, Abbye A.

1986 Researcher-writer. Barbara Coleman, producer-director. *A Walking Tour of St. Louis Cemeteries 1 and 2 of New Orleans.* Thirty minute video documentary. Wilson discusses the historic cemeteries from an architectural point of view. Features Henri Gandolfo. Broadcast on WLAE-TV, New Orleans, 31 October. Copy in WLAE-TV library.

1987 *A Guide To Photographic Collections In New Orleans.* Marie E. Windell, editor. New Orleans: Friends of the Earl K. Long Library and School of Urban and Regional Studies, University of New Orleans.

Hand, Stephen B.

1986 *Vieux Carré Commission Design Guidelines.* New Orleans: Vieux Carré Commission.

Louisiana Landmarks Society

1956 *Préservation*, newsletter for the Society.
t.d.

1990 "Reminiscences on the Founding and History of the Louisiana Landmarks Society on the Occasion of the Fortieth Anniversary". Unedited video tape, 13 September. Charles L. "Pie" Dufour and Samuel Wilson, Jr., speakers; James G. Derbes, moderator. Copy in Louisiana Landmarks Society Collection, Southeastern Architectural Archive.

MacDougall, Elisabeth Blair, editor

1990 *The Architectural Historian in America.* Washington, D.C.: National Gallery of Art.

Maddex, Diane, editor

1985 *All About Old Buildings, The Whole Preservation Catalog.* Washington, D.C.: The Preservation Press.

Watkin, David

1980 *The Rise Of Architectural History.* Chicago: The University of Chicago Press.

INDEX
(to the text)

The Louisiana Landmarks Society

The Louisiana Landmarks Society was established in 1950. However, its historic preservation advocacy activities began at the start of 1949 when members of the formative New Orleans chapter of the Society of Architectural Historians (an outgrowth of a history of Louisiana architecture course taught at Tulane University by Samuel Wilson, Jr.) banded together to save an early-nineteenth-century colonial Creole plantation, called the David Olivier House, from demolition. Leading the charge to preserve Gallier Hall in the 1950s and defeat the proposed Riverfront Expressway in the 1960s, Landmarks rapidly defined preservation advocacy in New Orleans. The current mission of the Louisiana Landmarks Society, the city and state's first historic preservation organization, is to promote historic preservation through education, advocacy, and operation of the Pitot House.

The values of the Louisiana Landmarks Society are manifested in the Pitot House, the nonprofit organization's home since 1964. This rare surviving example of colonial-era Creole architecture provides Landmarks with a site for exhibitions and educational programming that promote its preservation message. The historic structure and its interpreted grounds provide a transformative historic house tour experience for local and out-of-town visitors and provide the local public with a historically authentic and aesthetically idyllic setting for private functions.

The Louisiana Landmarks Society's major programs include an annual series of free public lectures on preservation topics, award recognition for outstanding preservation efforts, and the presentation of New Orleans' Nine Most Endangered properties—a program modeled after the National Trust for Historic Preservation's Eleven Most Endangered program.

In 1987, the board of trustees of the Louisiana Landmarks Society established a publication fund, named in honor of Samuel Wilson, Jr. The object of Landmarks' publication activity is to foster a more general interest in the architectural tradition of the region and to encourage publication of regional architectural history research. In the years since, Landmarks has published and marketed numerous monographs on architecture and preservation topics. By 2010, efforts to expand Landmarks' publishing program resulted in the creation of a publishing and distribution partnership with Pelican Publishing Company. Landmarks' share of proceeds from this partnership will support perpetuation of the Samuel Wilson, Jr. Publication Fund and its mission to provide for the development of future Louisiana Landmarks Society publications.

www.ingramcontent.com/pod-product-compliance
Lightning Source LLC
Chambersburg PA
CBHW031254090426
42742CB00007B/451